T0217115

Lecture Notes in Computer Science

Lecture Notes in Computer Science

Edited by G. Goos and J. Hartmanis

377

M. Gross D. Perrin (Eds.)

Electronic Dictionaries and Automata in Computational Linguistics

LITP Spring School on Theoretical Computer Science
Saint-Pierre d'Oléron, France, May 25–29, 1987
Proceedings

Springer-Verlag
Berlin Heidelberg New York London Paris Tokyo Hong Kong

Editors

Maurice Gross
Université Paris 7, LADL
2 place Jussieu, F-75251 Paris Cedex 05, France

Dominique Perrin
Université Paris 7, LITP
2 place Jussieu, F-75251 Paris Cedex 05, France

CR Subject Classification (1989): I.7, I.2.7, F.2.2

ISBN 3-540-51465-1 Springer-Verlag Berlin Heidelberg New York
ISBN 0-387-51465-1 Springer-Verlag New York Berlin Heidelberg

Printing and binding: Druckhaus Beltz, Hemsbach/Bergstr.
2145/3140-543210 – Printed on acid-free paper

Foreword

This volume gathers the texts of lectures given at the 15th Spring School in Theoretical Computer Science. This meeting was devoted to the relations between Formal Systems (automata, codes, grammars) and Natural Language Processing. It was organized jointly by M. Borillo, M. Gross, M. Nivat and D. Perrin and took place at Saint-Pierre d'Oléron in May 1987.

The two fields of Formal Systems and Natural Language Processing have strong historical links as exemplified by the joint work of N. Chomsky and M.P. Schützenberger[1] and the studies of Z. S. Harris on formalization[2] . Subsequently, they developed independently. Linguists stopped using elementary mathematical models either to characterize complete grammars or even to describe limited linguistic phenomena. They deepened their linguistic studies and built more specific formal representations. On their side, computer scientists have found a natural domain of application of formal systems in Compilation Theory and in the study of algorithms on strings[3].

With recent developments in text processing, the need for high performances is again bringing together the two fields. In the same way, since libraries can now contain all publications in their computer form, the large size of their collections requires sophisticated processing, even on the most powerful computers.

One basic component of linguistic systems is the dictionary look-up procedure : words of current texts have to be matched with the words of a given dictionary. For example, spelling checkers are based on this component. Many algorithmic questions then arise. They can be shaped according to specific applications and to the amount of information available about the texts and in the dictionaries. A nonexhaustive list is the following :

- fast string searching, with or without loss of information,
- fast searching of families of strings,
- coding texts and dictionaries in order to compact them,
- the use of large dictionaries of finite automata without loops for parsing,
- parsing of sentences of ambiguous languages,
- error correction in texts,
- the statistics on the distribution of words in texts.

The papers presented at the Spring School ranged from purely theoretical studies to detailed grammatical descriptions. Although a continuum of interests characterized the School, only

---

[1] Chomsky, N., Schützenberger M.-P. 1963 : The Algebraic Theory of Context-Free Languages, in *Computer Programming and Formal Systems*, P. Braffort and L. Hirschberg eds., North Holland Publishing Co.

[2] Z.S. Harris 1968 *Mathematical Structure of Language*, New York : Wiley Interscience.

[3] Aho, A., Sethi, R., Ullman, J. 1986 *Compilers, Principles and Tools*, Addison Wesley.

those papers which bore directly on computational issues have been included in the present volume. The other papers will be published in a special issue of *Lingvisticae Investigationes* (Amsterdam-Philadelphia : J. Benjamins) to appear in 1989.

Financial support came from the two **Programme de Recherches Coordonnées** *Mathématiques et Informatique* and *Informatique Linguistique* of the Ministry of Research and Higher Education, and from the *FIRTECH Industries de la langue* of the Ministry of Education. We express our thanks the three laboratories of the *CNRS* which helped in the organization of the meeting (*LADL* and *LITP* and *LSI* of Toulouse). Special mention of Mrs. Colette Ravinet for her perfect handling of all material questions has to be made.

Paris, January 1989   M. Gross, D. Perrin

Contents

Contents

Data Compression with Substitution*

Maxime Crochemore

Centre Scientifique et Polytechnique
Université de Paris-Nord
93430 Villetaneuse

1. Introduction.

The aim of data compression is to provide representations of data in a reduced form. The meaning of any data submitted to a compression process must not be changed. In other word, compression processes that we discuss are reversible.

Data compression techniques do not seem to be actually fashionable with those researchers working on very large texts. This is partially due to the recent introduction of new optical discs which bring a large amount of mass memory compared to the magnetic discs. However, data compression methods are interesting for their own and still applied to create archives or to deal with other kind of data such as images.

Besides, the second main interest for compressing data is to save time during their transmission. This is obviously true for communications between independent systems, specially with the development of local networks. But it is still true for the communication within a single system because graphic interfaces, for instance, lead to the transmission of large amount of data. Moreover, the cost of communication tend to increase while running time tend to decrease.

We describe data compression methods based on substitutions. Since the methods are general, they applies to data on which little is known. Semantic data compression techniques are not considered. So, compression ratios must be appreciate under that condition. The methods save about 50% memory space.

This work has been supported by PRC Math.-Info.

This paper is divided into three sections. In the first section we describe few elementar methods. Under some conditions they give good compression ratios. The second part of the paper is devoted to statistical encodings. The Unix (system V) command "pack" implement the famous Huffman's algorithm [Hu 51]. It admits a sequential version well suited for communication and implemented by the "compact" command of Unix (BSD 4.2).

The last section deals with the general problem of factor encoding. It contains the sequential algorithm of Ziv & Lempel [ZL 77]. The "compress" command od Unix (BSD 4.2) i based on a variant of this latter algorithm [We 84].

2. Substitutions.

The input of a data compression algorithm is a text. This text will be noted s, for **source** It is a sequence on the alphabet $\{0, 1\}$. The output of the algorithm is also a word of $\{0, 1\}$ denoted by c, for **encoded text**. Data compression methods that use substitutions are ofte described with the help of an intermediate alphabet A on which the source s translates into a **tex** t.. The method is then defined by the mean of two morphisms g and h from $A*$ into $\{0, 1\}*$. Th text t is an inverse image of s by the morphism g. The encoded text c is the direct imege of t b the morphism h. The set $\{(g(a), h(a)) / a \in A\}$, or simply the set $\{a, h(a)) / a \in A\}$ when th morphism g is implied, is called the **dictionary** of the coding method.

We only consider data compression methods without loss of information. This implie that a **decoding function** f exists such that $s=f(c)$. Furthermore, the morphism h is one-to-on which means that the set $\{h(a)) / a \in A\}$ is a **code** [BP 85].

The pair of morphisms, (g, h) leads to a classification of data compression methods wit substitution. We get four principal classes whether g is uniform (i.e. when all images of letter are words of the same length) or not, and whether the dictionary is fixed or computed during th compression process. Most elementary methods do not use a dictionary.

The efficiency of a compression method that encodes a text s into a text c, is mesured b the **compression ratio** $|s|/|c|$, where $|x|$ denotes the length of a text x. A great ratio means good compression.

	uniform morphism	non uniform
	differential encoding, topographic encoding	répétition encoding
fixed dictionary	statistical encoding (Huffman)	factor encoding
evolutive dictionary	sequential statistical encoding (Faller et Gallager)	Ziv and Lempel's algorithm

Basic methods.

1 Deletion of repetitions.

Let t be a text on the alphabet A. Let us assume, in this section, that t contain a certain quantity of repetitions made of some characters. Inside the text t, a sequence of n letter a ($a \in A$), an be replaced by

$$\& \, a \, n$$

where "&" is a new character which means that the following letter is repeted. This corresponds to the usual mathmatical notation a^n. When only one character is considered in that kind of ncoding, it does not need to appear after the "&". This is commonly done for "space deletion".

In pactice, the encoding of repetitions is done with an alphabet $\{0, 1\}^k$ with $k=7$ or 8. here is no problem in general to choose the character "&". In order to have a fast decoding lgorithm, the integer n is represented on k bits. More sophisticated integer representation is ossible but not suitable in the present situation. If $k=8$, the translation of a repetition of length ess than 256 has length 3. It is thus useless for a^2 and a^3, phenomenon which reduces the scope f the method.

2 Differential encoding.

Differential encoding is well understood when one wants to encode integers which belong o a narrow interval. Let, for instance,

$$(1981, 1982, 1980, 1982, 1985, 1984, 1984, 1981,...)$$

e a sequence of integers. It may be represented by the other sequence

$$(1981, 1, -2, 2, 3, -1, 0, -3,...).$$

hen, if all integers are encoded by their usual binary representations, the result is a word on the lphabet $\{0,1\}$ of smaller length than with the previous sequence.

More generally, a sequence $(u_1, u_2, ..., u_n)$ of data can be represented by the sequence of ifferences $(u_1, u_2-u_1, ..., u_n-u_{n-1})$ where "-" must be an appropriate operation.

Differential encoding is commonly used to create archives of successive versions of a ext. The initial text is fully memorized on the tape. For each following version, only the ifferences with its preceeding one is kept on the tape.

Another example of differential encoding, given in [He 86], works for telecopy. Pages to e transmitted are made of lines, each of 1728 bits. A differential encoding is first applied on onsecutive lines. So, if the nth line is

$$0101001 \; 0101010 \; 1001001 \; 1101001 \; 1011101 \; 1000000...$$

nd the $n+1^{th}$ line is

$$0101000\ 0101011\ 0111001\ 1100101\ 1011101\ 0000000...$$

the following line is to be sent

$$0000001\ 0000001\ 1110000\ 0001100\ 0000000\ 1000000...$$

In this latter line, runs of "1" are encoded by their length and its position within the line. Finally we get the sequence

$$(7,1),\quad (7,4),\quad (8,2),\quad (10,1),...$$

whose representation on the alphabet $\{0, 1\}$ is sent. Dense pages lead to small compression ratio. Best ratios are reached with blank (or black) pages.

3.3 Topographic representation.

The last elementary method that we mention in this paper is the topographic representation. It is well suited to encode texts consisting of characters scattered in a uniform environment. In topographic encoding method, additional words of bits are used to encode the positions of the significant characters of the text.

Assume, for instance, that the environment is composed of "-". Also assume 7-bit code words for characters. Then, each factor of length 7 of the text is translated into a word pw where p gives the positions of the characters of w within the factor. If 0101101 is the code-word for "-", the sequence of 7 characters "L-e----", that is,

$$1001100\ 0101101\ 1100101\ 0101101\ 0101101\ 0101101\ 0101101$$

is translated as

$$1010000\ 1001100\ 1100101$$

which is the sequence "PLe" (ASCII code). The code-word 1010000 of letter "P" determines the positions of "L" and "e" inside the source sequence. Decoding is thus easy to design.

The maximal compression ratio is 7. It is reached when the initial text is just composed of "-". The compression ratio is 7/8 when "-" does not occur in the text. In this latter case the compressed text is expanded!

4. Block encoding.

The most common technique to compress a text is to redefine the code-words associated to the letters of the alphabet. According to the pair of morphisms (g, h) introduced in section 2, this means that g gives the usual code attributed to the characters (ASCII or EBCDIC codes, for instance). Then, it remains to choose the morphism h in order to minimize the encoded text.

More generally, the morphism g is choosen uniform, which means that the images by g of the letters of A are all words of the same length. This is why they are often called **blocks**. In practice, this length is the length of the machine code-words of characters or twice more (i.e.

sually 7, 8, 14 or 16). On the contrary, the morphism h is not uniform in general because this vould decrease the power of the coding method. However, in order to have an efficient decoding lgorithm, images of h composed an instantaneous code, i.e. a **prefix code**: no word of the ode is a prefix of another one. This sort of encoding is called statistical since shortest images of tters correspond to most frequent letters within the initial text or within the class of considered xts.

.1 Huffman's method.

In 1951, Huffman gave a method to build prefix codes minimizing the length of ne encoded text. With each character a of the source text t on alphabet A, is associated the word (a) (on the alphabet $\{0, 1\}$) of the prefix code to determine. If the words $h(a)$ are arranged in a ee $\mathcal{A}$, leaves are in one-to-one correspondance with letters. The tree is binary (each node has xactly 0 or 2 sons) since one may easily verify that code $\{h(a) / a \in A\}$ is maximal for inclusion vhen the length $h(t)$ is minimal. The length $h(t)$ is equal to $\sum_{a \in A} n_a |h(a)|$ if n_a is the number f occurences of letter a inside text t. Let us define the weight of $\mathcal{A}$ as the sum $\sum_{f_a \in \mathcal{A}} n_a d(f_a)$ vhere $d(f_a)$ is the distance to the root of the leaf associated with the letter a. The determination of morphism h that minimizes the length $h(t)$ is then replaced by the construction of a tree of ninimal weight

[uffman's algorithm. Construction of minimal weight tree [Hu 51].
first consider the set $\{(f_a, n_a) / a \in A\}$ of leaves weighted by the number sof occurrences of tters;
give a common father to two leaves of minimal weight. Then, subtitute the elementary tree built nat way for the two leaves, and consider it as a new leaf, its weight being the sum of the weights f the two leaves.
stop the algorithm when there is only one leaf in the set.

Example : let $t = abracadabra$. The number of occurrences of letters are
$$n_a = 5, \quad n_b = 2, \quad n_c = 1, \quad n_d = 1, \quad n_r = 2.$$
he tree of the prefix code built by Huffman's algorithm is shown in the next figure. The words f $\{0,1\}*$ associated with letters a,b,c,d,r are :
$$h(a) = 0, \quad h(b) = 10, \quad h(c) = 1100, \quad h(d) = 1101, \quad h(r) = 111.$$
he translation of t on the alphabet $\{0,1\}$, $h(t)$, is then
$$0\ 10\ 111\ 0\ 1100\ 0\ 1101\ 0\ 10\ 111\ 0$$
vhich is a word of length 23. If the initial code-words of letters have length 5, we get a 55/23 = .4 compression ratio. However, if these code-words have to be memorized together with the

tree structure, the translation contains 35 more bits. The compression ratio is thus reduced to 55/58 = 0.95.

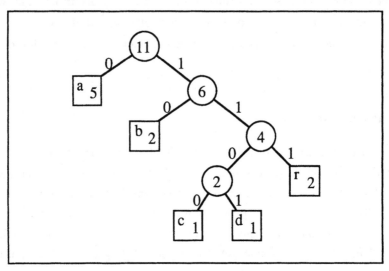

Huffman's tree for *abracadabra*.

The above algorithm needs the quantities n_a , numbers of occurrences of letters that appear in the source text t. The output of the algorithm is a morphism h fully adapted to t. This morphism must be known at the decoding phase. So, morphism h must be memorized in the same time as the encoded text $h(t)$. The same remark holds for morphism g. This phenomenon does not strongly affects the compression ratio because the structure of the binary tree of the prefix code can be represented with $2|A|+1$ bits.

The main default of Huffman's algorithm is that the source text must be read twice. The first time to compute the frequences of the letters and the second time to encode the text. Only one reading of the text is possible if one uses average frequences in relation with the class of texts to compress. In that latter situation, the algorithm does not insure, of course, that the encoded text has minimal length according to the conditons of the method.

Assume that each letter a of A has probability p_a to occur in the considered texts. The **entropy** of the code $X=\{h(a) \ / \ a \in A\}$ is the quantity

$$H(X) = -\sum_{a\in A} p_a \log_2(p_a)$$

expressed in bits.

The entropy is a lower bound to the average length $m(X)$ of the code-words $h(a)$:

$$m(X) = \sum_{a\in A} p_a \ |h(a)| .$$

The equality $H(X)=m(X)$ is only satisfied when, for each letter a of A, $p_a = 2^{-|h(a)|}$. The ratio $H(X)/m(X)$ measures the efficiency of the code.

In French, the entropy of letters is sligthly less than 4 bits. The efficiency of a Huffman code is more than 99%. The Morse code is also a prefix code by the correspondence

— 11, - 1, space between dot and line 0, end of letter 00.

ts efficiency is 66%. In English, the entropy of letters is weakly more then 4 bits. The efficiency of a Huffman code is close to 99% and the one of the Morse code is better than in French.

Finally, it must be noted that Huffman's method generally behaves better when it is pplied to digrams instead of letters.

.2 Sequential algorithm.

In the seventies, Faller [Fa 73] and Gallager [Ga 78] independently designed a sequential ata compression algorithm based on Huffman's method. With this algorihm, the source text is ead only once. Moreover, the memory space required by the algorithm is proportional to the size f the tree of section 4.1. The encoding of the letters of the source text is realised at the same time he text is read. In some situations, the compression ration is even better than the ratio of Iuffman's method.

We define a **weighted tree** as a binary tree whose nodes are weighted by an integer unction p such that: if x is an internal node, $p(x)$ is the sum of the weigths of its two sons. A veigthed tree of minimal weigth is called a **Huffman tree**. It is a weighted tree $\mathcal{A}$ that ninimizes the sum $\sum_{f_a \in \mathcal{A}} n_a\, d(f_a)$ where f_a runs through the leaves of $\mathcal{A}$. Huffman's lgorithm builds such a tree.

We now describe the sequential data compression algorithm. Assume that text t has lready been encoded and that an Huffman tree $\mathcal{H}(t)$ has been built according to the frequencies f the letters in t. The code-word associated with the next letter a is then given by the tree $\mathcal{H}(t)$. fterwards, the tree is transformed to get a Huffman tree $\mathcal{H}(ta)$ for ta. At decoding time the tree volves according to the same algorithm. The reason why this method is practicable is that pdating the Huffman tree can be implemented in time proportional to the transmitted code-word. his means a real-time data compression algorithm. Moreover, the compression ratio is close to hat of Huffman's method.

The key-point of the sequential algorithm is a characterization of Huffman trees.

iblings property. Let $\mathcal{A}$ be a tree weigthed by a function p whose values are strictly positive ntegers. Then, $\mathcal{A}$ is a Huffman tree iff its nodes can be ordered in a sequence $(x_1\text{-}x_2,...,x_{2n-1})$ such that:

_ the weight sequence $(p(x_1),p(x_2),...,p(x_{2n-1}))$ is increasing,

_ for any i ($1 \le i < n$), the consecutive nodes x_{2i-1} et x_{2i} are siblings (they have the same father).

Huffman's algorithm considers the nodes of the tree it builds in an ordering which satisfies the above two points. Siblings property can be proved by induction on the number of leaves of the tree. The characterization remains true if only one leaf has a null weight.

During the sequential encoding, the transformation of $\mathcal{H}(t)$ into $\mathcal{H}(ta)$ starts by the incrementation of the weight of the leaf x_i that corresponds to a. If the point 1 of the sibling property is no longer satisfied after incrementation, node x_i is exchanged with the node x_j for which j is the greatest integer such that $p(x_j)<p(x_i)$. If necessary, the same operation is repeated on the father of x_i and so on. The exchange of nodes is, in fact, the exchange of the corresponding subtrees. The tree structure is not affected by exchanges because weights strictly increase from the leaves to the root.

It remains to explain the behaviour of the algorithm when a new letter a is encountered. The algorithm maintains a leaf of null weight associated with all the letters that have not already appeared. The translation of the letter a is composed by the path from the root to the null weighted leaf, for the one part, and by the initial code-word $g(a)$ (ASCII code of a, for instance) for the other part. Then, the null weighted leaf is replaced by an elementary tree as shown in the next figure.

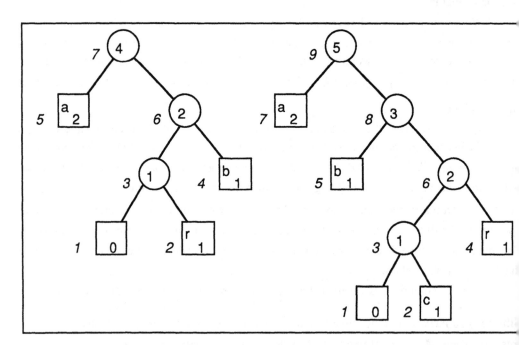

Example. The above figure shows how $\mathcal{H}(abra)$ is changed into $\mathcal{H}(abrac)$. The number besides nodes give an ordering satisfying the siblings property.

Example. The next figure shows the sequential encoding of *abracadabra*.

Letters are assumed to be initially encoded on 5 bits ($a \to 00000$, $b \to 00001$, $c \to$ 0010, ..., $z \to 11010$). The entire translation of *abracadabra* is :

        00000 000001 0010001 0 10000010 0 110000011 0 110 110 0

          a   *b*   *r*   *a*   *c*   *a*   *d*   *a* *b* *r* *a*

We get a word of length 45. These 45 bits are to be compared with the 58 bits obtained by Huffman's algorithm. In that case, the sequential algorithm gives a better compression ratio, say 5/45 = 1,22.

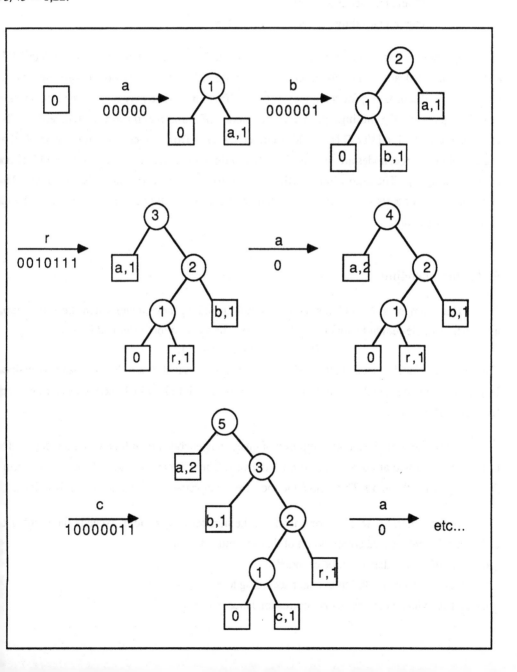

Empirical tests. Here are some compression ratios obtained with a sequential statistical algorithm on 100K-character texts [Kn 85].

Grimm's tales

Character encoding (7 bits)	1.6
Digram encoding (14 bits)	1.8

Technical book

Character encoding (7 bits)	1.3
Digram encoding (14 bits)	1.5

The precise analysis of sequential statistical data compression has been done by Vitter [V 87]. The analysis leads him discover an even better algorithm. The idea of the improvement is to choose a specific ordering for the nodes of the Huffman tree. One may note indeed that, in the ordering given by the siblings property, two nodes of same weight are exchangeable. The ordering considered in [Vi 87] is a width-first tree-traversal from leaves to the root. Moreover, at each level in the tree, nodes are ordered form left to right and leaves of weight p preceed internal nodes of weight p. The algorithm is efficient even for texts of few thousands characters. The encoding of larger texts with Vitter's algorithm save almost one bit per character compared with Huffman's algorithm.

5. Factor encoding.

Data compression methods with substitution find all their power when the substitution applies to variable-length factors instead of blocks. The substitution is defined by a dictionary:
$$D = \{(f, c) / f \in F, c \in C\}.$$
The set F is, a priori, a set of factors of the source text s. It satisfies $s \in F^*$. The set C contained in $\{0, 1\}^*$ is a code. Finally, D defines a function from C into F, which extends to a morphism from $\{0, 1\}^*$ into F^*.

Example. Let t be a text composed of characters encoded on 8 bits. One may choose for C the 8-bit words that correspond to no letter of t. Then, F can be a set of factors occurring frequently inside the text t. This amount to increase the alphabet on which the text t is written.

In the general case of factor encoding, the number of questions exceeds the number of efficient solutions. A data compression of that sort must describe
_ the set F of factors that are to be encoded,
_ the method to factorize the source text according to F,
_ the code C which is in one-to-one correspondance with F.

When the text is given, the computation of an optimal such encoding is a NP-complete problem [St 77]. The proof can be done inside the following model of encoding. Let A be the alphabet on which s is written, and let n the length of s. The encoding of s is a word of the form $d\&c$ where d ($\in A^*$) is supposed to represent the dictionary, $\&$ is a new letter (not in A), and c is the compressed text. The part c of the encoding is written on the alphabet $A \cup \{1, 2,..., n\} \times \{1, ..., n\}$. A pair (i, j) that appears inside c means a reference to the factor of length j of d that occurs at position i.

Example. On $A = \{a, b, c\}$, let $s = aababbabbabbc$. Its encoding can be $babb\&aa(1,4)a(0,5)c$. The explicit dictionary is then
$$D = \{(babb, \ (1, 4)), (bbabb, \ (0, 5))\} \cup A \times A.$$

Inside the above model, the length of $d\&c$ is the number of occurrences of both letters and pairs of integers that appear in it. This length is 12 in the previous example. The search for a shortest word $d\&c$ that encodes a given text s reduces to the SCS-problem (find the shortest common superstring of a finite set of words) which is a classical NP-complete problem.

.1 Fixed dictionary.

When the set F of factors is known, the main problem becomes the factorization of the source text s according to the elements of F:
$$s = f_1 f_2 ... f_k \quad \text{with} \quad f_1, f_2, .. f_k \in F.$$
It is important that the integer k be as small as possible, and the factorization is said to be optimal when k is minimal.

The simplest strategy to factorize s is to use a greedy algorithm. The factorization is computed sequentially. The first factor f_1 is the longest prefix of s that belongs to F. The decomposition of the rest of the text is done iteratively in the same way.

Note 1: if F is a set of letters or digrams (F included in $A \cup A \times A$), the greedy algorithm computes an optimal factorization. The condition may seem quite restrictive, but in French, for instance, the most frequent factors ("er", "en") have length 2.

Note 2: if F is a factorial set (all factors of words of F are in F), the greedy algorithm computes an optimal factorization.

Another factorization strategy is found in [HR 84]. Its time complexity is similar to the previous strategy, but it leads to optimal factorizations under wider conditions.

Semigreedy algorithm.

_ let $m = \max\{|uv| / u, v \in F$ and uv prefix of $s\}$. Then, the first element f_1 of the factorizatio belongs to F and satisfies:

there exists $v \in F, f_1v$ prefix of s, and $|f_1v| = m$.

_ let $s = f_1s'$. The same process is iterated on s'.

Example. Let $F = \{a, b, c, ab, ba, bb, bab, bba, babb, bbab\}$ and $s = aababbabbabbc$ The greedy algorithm produces the factorization

$$s = a\ ab\ ab\ babb\ ab\ b\ c$$

which has 7 factors. The semigreedy algorithm gives

$$s = a\ a\ ba\ bbab\ babb\ c$$

which is an optimal factorization. Note that F is prefixial.

Proposition. If the set F is prefixial (all prefixes of words of F are in F), the semigreed algorithm produces an optimal factorization.

When the set F is finite, the semigreedy algorithm may be realized by the string-matchin algorithm of Aho & Corasick [AC 75]. This leads to a linear time algorithm to factorize the text s

The next step in the compression process is the determination of the code-words of the se C. As in statistical encoding, the choice of code-words associated with factors of F may take int account the frequencies of the factors. This choice can be done once for all, or in a dynamic wa during the factorization of s.

An example of dynamic factor encoding is given in [BSTW 86]. The set is predefine The words $f (\in F)$ of the factorization of the source text are put in a list as soon as they a encoutered in s. The code-word c associated with f is its index in the list. If f is not already in th list, c is the length of the list. Then, the word f is put or shift ed at the front end of the list. Doin so, frequent factors tend to be encoded by short integers.

5.2 Evolutive dictionary.

In 1977, Ziv et Lempel [ZL 77] introduced a data compression method which does n need a prior computation of the set F of factors of s. The dictionary is built in the same time a the text is read. As in the schema of [BSTW 86], the code-words are the indices of factors in th dictionary. So, we regard the dictionary D as a sequence of words $(f_0, f_1, ...)$.

iv & Lempel's algorithm.

initialize D to $\{e\}$ (e is the empty word); initialize x to s;

repeat the four instructions until x is empty:

    _ let f_k be the longest word of D such that $x = f_k\, a\, y$ with $a \in A$;

    _ output the index k on $lg|D|$ bits;

    _ output the initial code-word of letter a on $lg|A|$ bits;

    _ add the word $f_k a$ at the rear end of D, and substitute y for x.

he function lg is defined by: $lg(1)=1$ and, for $n>1$, $lg(n)$ is the ceiling of $\log_2(n)$.

xample. Let $A = \{a, b, c\}$. Assume that the initial code-words of letters are 00 for a, 01 for

and 10 for c. Let $s = aababbabbabbc$. Then, the decomposition of s is

$$s = a\ ab\ abb\ abba\ b\ bc$$

hich leads to

$$c = 000\ 101\ 1001\ 1100\ 00001\ 10110.$$

fter that, the dictionary D contains the 7 words:

$$D = (e, a, ab, abb, abba, b, bc).$$

    The main improvement on the above algorithm is to put into the initial dictionary all the

ssible characters (ASCII characters for instance). This version has been designed and studied

[MW 84], [Ja 85] and [We 84]. Welch's algorithm is the base of the command "compress"

ailable under Unix (BSD 4.2).

    Since the dictionary built by the above algorithm is prefixial, the semigreedy factorization

gorithm may help to reduce the number of factors in the decomposition [HR 84]. Each word

lded to the dictionary spends a constant memory space because the dictionary is, in fact, a tree.

hen it has reached its maximal size it may be fixed or reset.

    The model of encoding valid for that kind of compression method is more general than

e preceeding one. The source text s is a sequence of length n on the alphabet A, and its

coding c is on the alphabet $A \cup \{1,2,..,n\} \times \{1,2,..,n\}$. The pairs (i,j) occurring in c are

ferences of factors of s itself: i is the position of the factor, and j is its length.

    Example. Let again $s = aababbabbabbc$. It can be encoded into

$$c = a\ (0,1)b\ (1,2)b\ (3,3)a\ b\ (11,1)c,$$

length 10, which corresponds to Ziv & Lempel's algorithm.

    The number of factors of the decomposition of the source text reduces if we consider its

factorization. The **f-factorisation** of s is a sequence of words $(f_1, f_2,..., f_m)$ such that

$= f_1 f_2 .. f_m$, and iteratively defined by:

    f_i is the shortest prefix of $f_i f_{i+1} ... f_m$ which occurs here for the first time.

Example. The f-factorization of $s = aababbabbabbc$ is

$$(a, ab, abb, abbabbc)$$

which accounts to encode s into

$$c = a \ (0,1)b \ (1,2)b \ (3,6)c,$$

word of length 7 only.

The integer m of the f-factorization $(f_1, f_2, ..., f_m)$ acts as a measure of the complexity of the text s. The compression ratio reached with f-factorizations has been shown to be optimal as texts become longer. The running time of the computation of f-factorizations is linear in the length of the text, if one calls on the construction of the suffix-tree of s [RPE 81] or the construction of the suffix automaton of s [Cr 86].

Empirical tests. Welch gives in [We 84] compression ratios obtained with a variant of Ziv & Lempel' algorithm on texts of size varying from 1 to 10 Mbytes.

English text	1.8
Technical document	2.1
Cobol sources	2 to 6
Program sources	2.3
Object codes	1.5
Array of real numbers	1.0

6. Conclusion.

All the data compression methods described in this paper are based on substitutions acting on characters or factors occurring inside the source texts. The average expected compression ratio is often close to 2. Most methods have a bad behaviour when error appears in encoded texts. One bit lost and the decompression is almost impossible!

To increase the compression ratios, other methods can be used. Arithmetic coding is such an example which leads to higher efficiency.

Another way to increase the compression ratios is to give up the "lossless information" condition. These compaction methods must use semantic rule to recover the original information. Such methods cannot be applied to create archives or to communicate. A compaction example is found in [McI 82] for the "spell" program available under the Unix operating system.

. **References.**

AC 75] A.V.AHO, M.J.CORASICK, Efficient string matching: An aid to bibliographic research, *Commun. ACM* **18,6** (1975), 333-340.

BSTW 86] J.L.BENTLEY, D.D.SLEATOR, R.E.TARJAN, V.K.WEI, A locally adaptive data compression scheme, *Commun. ACM* **29,4** (1986), 320-330.

BP 85] J.BERSTEL, D.PERRIN, *Theory of codes*, Academic Press (1985).

Cr 86] M.CROCHEMORE, Transducers and Repetitions, *Theoret. Comput. Sci.* **45** (1986), 63-86.

El 75] P.ELIAS, Universal Codeword Sets and Representation of the Integers, *I.E.E.E. Trans. Inform. Theory* **IT 21,2** (1975), 194-203.

Fa 73] N.FALLER, An adaptive system for data compression, in *Record of the 7th Asilomar Conference on Circuits, Systems, and Computers* (1973), 593-597.

Ga 68] R.G.GALLAGER, *Information Theory and Reliable Communication*, Wiley (1968).

Ga 78] R.G.GALLAGER, Variations on a theme by Huffman, *I.E.E.E. Trans. Inform. Theory* **IT 24,6** (1978), 668-674.

GM 82] E.N.GILBERT, C.L.MONMA, Multigram Codes, *I.E.E.E. Trans. Inform. Theory* **IT 28,2** (1982), 346-348.

HR 84] A.HARTMAN, M.RODEH, Optimal Parsing of Strings, in *(Combinatorial Algorithms on Words, Apostolico & Galil ed., Springer-Verlag* (1985)) 155-167.

Ha 80] R.W.HAMMING, *Coding and Information Theory*, Prentice-Hall (1980).

He 87] G.HELD, *La compression des données, méthodes et applications*, Masson (1987).

Hu 51] D.A.HUFFMAN, A method for the construction of minimum redundancy codes, *Proc. IRE* **40** (1951), 1098-1101.

Ja 85] M.JAKOBSSON, Compression of character strings by an adaptive dictionary, *BIT* **25** (1985), 593-603.

Kn 85] D.E.KNUTH, Dynamic Huffman Coding, *J. Algorithms* **6** (1985), 163-180.

La 83] G.G.LANGDON JR., A Note on the Ziv-Lempel Model for Compressing Individual Sequences, *I.E.E.E. Trans. Inform.Theory* **IT 29,2** (1983), 284-287.

LZ 76] A.LEMPEL, J.ZIV, On the Complexity of Finite Sequences, *I.E.E.E. Trans. Inform.Theory* **IT 22,1** (1976), 75-81.

Ll 87] J.A.LLEWELLYN, Data Compression for a Source with Markov Charateristics, *Comput. J.* **30,2** (1987), 149-156.

Mc 82] M.D.MCILROY, Development of a Spelling List, *I.E.E.E. Trans. Commun.* **COM 30,1** (1982), 91-99.

MW 84] V.S.MILLER, M.N.WEGMAN, Variations on a Theme by Ziv and Lempel, in *(Combinatorial Algorithms on Words, Apostolico & Galil ed., Springer-Verlag* (1985), 131-140.

[RL 79] J.RISSANEN, G.G.LANGDON JR., Arithmetic Coding, *IBM J. Res. Dev.* **23,2** (1979), 149-162.

[RL 81] J.RISSANEN, G.G.LANGDON JR., Universal Modeling and Coding, *I.E.E.E. Trans Inform.Theory* **IT 27,1** (1981), 12-23.

[RPE 81] M.RODEH, V.R.PRATT, S.EVEN, Linear Algorithm for Data Compression via String Matching, *J. Assoc. Comput. Mach.* **28,1** (1981), 16-24.

[St 84] J.A.STORER, Textual Substitution Techniques for Data Compression, in (*Combinatoric Algorithms on Words, Apostolico & Galil ed., Springer-Verlag* (1985)) 111-129.

[SS 82] J.A.STORER, T.G.SZYMANSKI, Data Compression via Textual Substitution, *J. Assoc Comput. Mach.* **29,4** (1982), 928-951.

[Vi 87] J.S.VITTER, Design and Analysis of Dynamic Huffman Codes, *J. Assoc. Compu Mach.* **34,4** (1987), 825-845.

[We 84] T.A.WELCH, A Technique for High-Performance Data Compression, *I.E.E.I Computer* **17,6** (1984), 8-19.

[WNC 87] I.H.WITTEN, R.M.NEAL, J.G.CLEARY, Arithmetic coding for data compressio *Commun. ACM* **30,6** (1987), 520-540.

[ZL 77] J.ZIV, A.LEMPEL, A Universal Algorithm for Sequential Data Compression, *I.E.E.I Trans. Inform.Theory* **IT 23,3** (1977), 337-343.

[ZL 78] J.ZIV, A.LEMPEL, Compression of Individual Sequences via Variable-rate Codin *I.E.E.E. Trans. Inform.Theory* **IT 24,5** (1978), 530-536.

Some Pronominalization Issues
in generation of texts in Romance languages

Laurence DANLOS
LADL , Université de Paris 7
2 Place Jussieu, 75251 Paris Cedex 07

Introduction

In a man-machine dialogue in natural language, a generation system produces the answers of the machine. A generation system is the counterpart of an analysis system which interprets the messages of the user.

The machine answers must 1) give the user the information he is expecting for, 2) formulate this information in a consistent style. These two tasks give raise to the following components of a generation system : a reasonning module (expert system) deals with the **What to say?** question and returns a semantic representation of the information that is to be conveyed to the user; this semantic representation is translated into a text by a linguistic generation component which deals with the **How to say it?** question. This paper is concerned only with the linguistic generation component.

It is generally believed that a linguistic generation component can be modularized into a sequence of modules, the first one making the conceptual decisions (e.g. ordering of the information), the following ones making the linguistic decisions (e.g. lexical and syntactic construction choices), the penultimate one performing the syntactic operations (e.g. subject-verb agreement), and the last one handling the morphological operations (e.g. conjugation of verbs). Given that "high level" decisions must be made before "low level" decisions, this way of modularizing a linguistic generation component relies on the following hypotheses:

conceptual decisions are "high level" decisions, linguistic decisions are "low level" , syntactic operations are very low level and morphological operations are even lower level than the syntactic ones.

Our previous work has brought these hypotheses into question to the extent that we have shown in (L. Danlos 1985, 1987a) that the conceptual and linguistic decisions are operations that depend on each other, none being "higher" than the other ones. Therefore, we designed a generation model modularized into a "strategic component" and a "syntactic component". The strategic component makes the conceptual and linguistic decisions simultaneously, as briefly presented in 2. It gives back a "text template" which is a list of the form:

$$(S1 \; Punct1 \; S2 \; Punct2 \; ... \; Si \; Puncti \; ... \; Sn \; Punctn)$$

where Puncti is a punctuation sign and Si a sentence template. The sentence template underlying the sentence

(1)   *Ugo shot Mary and she was killed.*

is:

S1 (:COORD-S   (:coord-conj *and*)
                (:Cl (:subject HUM1) (:verb *shoot* (:tense past)) (:dir-object HUM2))
                (:Cl (:subject HUM2) (:verb *kill* (:tense past)(:voice passive)))))

where HUM1 and HUM2 are tokens with the following definitions:

HUM1 =: PERSON	HUM2 =: PERSON
NAME : Ugo	NAME : Maria
SEX : masc	SEX : fem

Text templates are synthesized into texts by the syntactic component. On the one hand, this component synthesizes the tokens, e.g. it determines for each occurence of HUM2 in S1 if it should be synthesized as a reflexive pronoun, a personal pronoun or a noun group and it produces the corresponding form. On the other hand, the syntactic component performs syntactic operations such as the subject-verb agreement, or the reduction of a sentential clause into an infinitive clause (L. Danlos 1987b).

We are going here to concentrate on some pronominalization issues. First, we are going to show that pronominalization involves the morphological level for the generation systems that produce texts in Romance languages. The decisions concerning pronominalization, which is a stumbling block for natural language processing, must certainly not be made last. Thus, the morphological level (level supposedly very "low") must not be taken into account only at the very last stage of the generation process.

Second, we will go one step further in our research that aims at showing the interaction of decisions in text generation. We will show that our modularization into two components - a strategic component and a syntactic component, the latter handling pronominalization - is even too modular: some pronominalization questions should be taken into account while the conceptual or linguistic decisions are made.

2 Brief presentation of the strategic component

The strategic component relies upon a linguistic data base that we have called "discourse grammar". A discourse grammar establishes a mapping between a type of semantic relationship (i.e. a causal relation) and the list of discourse structures enabling it to be expressed. Our notion of discourse grammar[1] integrates decisions on 1) the ordering of information, 2) the linearization into sentences (namely, the choice between juxtaposition, subordination, relativization or coordination as a sentence linearization procedure), 3) the form of the sentences (namely, the choice between the active, passive or ergative construction[2]). An example of discourse structure for causal relation is:

(A) (active <CAUSE>) and (passive-without-agent <RESULT>).

where <CAUSE> and <RESULT> stand for the sentences that will express respectively the cause and the result. The discourse *Ugo shot Mary and she was killed* is of structure (A). In this discourse, the cause preceeds the result, the linearization mode is coordination with the conjunction *and* , the cause is expressed in the active and the result in the passive without agent. Another example of discourse structure for causal relation is:

(B) (active <CAUSE>) . (ergative <RESULT>) .
=: *Ugo knocked over the glass. It broke.*

The strategic component selects a discourse structure in the appropriate discourse grammar. This operation amounts in making simultaneously conceptual and some linguistic decisions. The other linguistic decision that is made by the strategic component is the lexical choices for verbs, more precisely, for predicative elements. The lexical choices and the selection of a discourse structure are also operations that depend on each other. For example, the selection of the discourse structure (B) is uncompatibe with choosing *kill* to express the result since this verb cannot undergo the ergative transformation. As a consequence, the following discourse of structure (B) is unacceptable: **Ugo shot Mary. She killed.*

3 Presentation of the syntactic component

A sentence is either a coordination of sentences (COORD-S) or a clause (Cl). A simplified version of the clause template syntax is the following one [3] :

---

[1] Other researchers in text generation make use of a "discourse grammar", for example (K. McKeown 1985). However, her notion of discourse grammar gives only guidelines on the order of the information, thus is used only for conceptual decisions.
[2] The passive construction is examined both with and without agent. The ergative transformation when applied to the clause *Ugo broke the glass* gives back *The glass broke.*
[3] A more complete version of the text and clause template syntax is given in (L. Danlos 1987b). It includes representations for subordination, attributes, adverbial phrases, and so on. A clause template may represent a clause in the passive : the [subject] is then the surface subject, the verb being marked as having to be conjugated at the passive voice.

[Cl] = (:Cl [subject] [verb] cplt$n$ ($0 \leq n \leq 2$))
[subject] = (:subject token)
[verb] = (:verb *verb*)
cplt = [dir-object] / [à-object] / [de-object] / [loc-object] /[prép-object]
[dir-object] = (:dir-object token)
[à-object] = (:à-object token)
[de-object] = (:de-object token)
[loc-object] = (:loc-object [loc] (:object token))
[prép-object] = (:prép-object [prép] (:object token))
[loc] = (:loc *locative-preposition*)
[prép] = (:prép *preposition*)

The prepositional complements [à-object], [de-object] and [loc-object] are complements respectively introduced by:
-*à* , *de*   and a locative preposition in French
- *a* , *di* and a locative preposition in Italian.
They are separated from the prepositional complements [prép-object] introduced by other prepositions because they have a specific syntactic behaviour, especially in regard to pronominalization (see section 4).

Consider the following clause template:

(:Cl (:subject HUM1) (:verb *amare* (:tense present)) (:dir-object HUM2))
with

HUM1 =: PERSON	HUM2 =: PERSON
NAME : Ugo	NAME : Maria
SEX : masc	SEX : fem

According to the context (i.e. the clause templates that have been previously synthesized), the Italian syntactic component synthesizes it as one of the following clauses :

Ugo ama Maria	(Ugo loves Mary)
Ugo l'ama	(Ugo loves her)
Ama Maria	(He loves Mary)
L'ama	(He loves her)
Quest'uomo ama questa donna	(This man loves this woman)
Quest'uomo l'ama	(This man loves her)
Ama questa donna	(He loves this woman)

In a generation system producing texts in Romance languages, a syntactic component has to handle three different orders for the synthesis of a clause:
- the order of the elements in the clause template that is to be synthesized,
- the order in which the elements of the clause template must be synthesized,
- the order in which the synthesized elements must be placed in the final clause.

3.1 The order of the elements in the clause template that is to be synthesized

We will suppose that this order corresponds to the canonical order of a clause, i. e. :
subject - verb - direct object - indirect object(s)

3.2 The order in which the elements of the clause template must be synthesized

This order is determined by "non local dependencies" which are to be found when the synthesis of an element X depends upon that of another element Y. Such a dependency requires the synthesis of X to be carried out after that of Y, whatever the order of X and Y in the clause template and whatever their order in the final synthesized clause. Moreover, cases of "cross dependencies" are to be found when the synthesis of X depends upon that of Y and when the synthesis of Y depends upon that of X. A cross dependency leads to conflicting orderings, namely synthesis of X after that of Y and synthesis of Y after that of X. The solution to such conflicting orderings is to perform a sequence of incomplete syntheses of X and Y. To illustrate non local and cross dependencies, let us consider the synthesis of the verb and direct object in French.

a) The synthesis of the verb depends upon that of the [dir-object] for two reasons. First, there is a switch from the auxiliary *avoir* to the auxiliary *être* (when the verb is conjugated in a compound tense) if the [dir-object] is synthesized as a reflexive pronoun (which must appear before the verb):

Ugo a détesté Marie	(Ugo hated Mary)
Ugo s'est détesté	(Ugo hated himself)

Second, there is agreement in gender and number between the past participle of a verb conjugated in a compound tense and a [dir-object] synthesized as a personal pronoun (which must appear before the verb):

Ugo, je l'ai détesté	(Ugo, I hated him)
Marie, je l'ai détestée	(Mary, I hated her)

b) The synthesis of the [dir-object] depends upon that of the verb in the following way, which will be explained in detail in 4.1 and 4.2: determining whether the [dir-object] has to be synthesized as a personal pronoun may depend upon the first letter of the conjugated verb.

c) All in all, the synthesis of the verb depends upon that of the [dir-object] and the synthesis of the [dir-object] depends upon that of the verb. This cross dependency can be handled with the following sequence of incomplete syntheses:

1) Determine if the [dir-object] must be synthesized as a reflexive pronoun (by checking if its value is equal to the value of the subject). If it is, mark the verb as having to be conjugated with the auxiliary *être*

2) Synthesize the verb (i.e. conjugate it) without taking into account a possible agreement between a past participle and a pronominalized [dir-object]. In Step 2, the verb is conjugated in a compound tense with the right auxiliary thanks to Step 1. Let us mention that the conjugation of a verb is a morphological operation.

3) Synthesize the [dir-object] if it has not been synthesized as a reflexive pronoun in Step 1. In Step 3 the form of the conjugated verb provided by Step 2 is used to determine if the [dir-object] has to be synthesized as a personal pronoun (see Sections 4.1 and 4.2).

4) Complete the synthesis of the verb if necessary, i.e. carry out the agreement in gender and number between a past participle if any (information given by Step 2) and a pronominalized [dir-object] if any (infomation given by Step 3).

These four steps imply that both the direct object and the verb have to be checked over twice. Note that these checkings are for the synthesis of these two elements only. The cross dependencies that arise from other elements (see Section 4.1) imply that the direct object and the verb have to be checked over more than twice. Generally speaking, a clause template (i.e. a tree) is gone through several times in the syntactic component processes.

3.3 The order in which the synthesized elements must be placed in the final clause

This order is determined by syntactic transformations that move synthesized elements. For example, the "length permutation transformation" moves a direct object after an indirect object when the former is "longer" than the latter:

I bought a book about Napoleon which was published in 1924 from this bookseller
--> *I bought from this bookseller a book about Napoleon which was published in 1924*

Another example of such a syntactic transformation is the English "dative transformation" illustrated in the following pair:

> *John gave a book to Mary*
--> *John gave Mary a book*

The dative transformation cannot take place if the direct object is pronominalized:

> *John gave it to Mary*
--> **John gave Mary it*

The decision to apply the dative transformation to a clause should therefore be made after the synthesis of the direct object.

4 Synthesis of personal pronouns[4]

If a token refers to the speaker(s) or the hearer(s), it must be synthesized as a first or second person pronoun. The only operation to be performed is then the computation of this "dialogue" pronoun. Otherwise, we consider synthesizing a token as a third person personal pronoun only if it has already been synthesized (because occuring in a previous clause template, for example). In other words, we do not consider the left pronominalization phenomena (T. Reinhart 1983). Determining whether a token which does not refer to the speaker(s) or hearer(s) and which has already been synthesized has to be synthetized as a pronoun requires the following steps to be gone through[5]:

1) Compute the form of the foreseen pronoun.
2) Compute the list L1 of tokens that have been synthesized in nominal phrases the "morphological" features (i.e. gender and number) of which are compatible with the form of the foreseen pronoun provided by Step 1.
3) Compute the sublist L2 of L1 that contains the elements that are syntactically compatible with the foreseen pronoun.
4) Compute the sublist L3 of L2 that contains the elements that are semantically compatible with the foreseen pronoun.
5) According to the number of elements in L3, and maybe according to other considerations, decide if actually the foreseen pronoun has to be synthesized.

---

[4] This section has been written with F. Namer. Some parts of it are published in (L. Danlos and F. Namer 1988).
[5] Steps 2,3,4 and 5 are the ones an analysis system should go through when searching the referent of a third person pronoun.

4.1 Computation of the form of the foreseen pronoun

This computation involves the following factors :

1) The syntactic position in which the token that could be synthesized as a pronoun appears. In English, it is enough to distinguish between the subject and complement positions. In French and Italian, it is necessary to distinguish between the [subject], [dir-object], [à-object], [de-object], [loc-object] and [prép-object] positions. On the one hand, the [subject] and [prép-object] positions give generally rise to pronouns that are similar to the English ones[6]. On the other hand, the other positions may give rise to pronouns that must stand before the verb, such pronouns being noted *Ppv* ("pronoms pré-verbaux").

2) The person and number of the token. Person and number are semantic information which are given in the definition of the token.

3) The gender of the nominal phrase that synthesizes the previous occurrence of the token. In French and Italian languages, which have only the masculine and feminine gender, gender is not semantic but lexical information. Consider the token TOK1 with the following definition :

> TOK1 =: BICYCLE
> NUMBER : 1
> DEFINITE : yes

In French, it can be synthesized as a feminine noun group *la bicyclette* (the bicycle) or as a masculine noun group *le vélo* (the bike) . The gender of a pronoun which synthesizes a token is generally equal to the gender of the previous occurrence of the token :

> *La bicyclette est cassée. (Elle + * Il) est au garage.*   (The bicycle is broken. It is at the garage.)
> *Le vélo est cassé. (Il + * Elle) est au garage.*   (The bike is broken. It is at the garage.)

4) The human nature of the token along with the verb (in the infinitive form) of the clause template. As an example, let us consider the synthesis of an [à-object] in Italian. The verbs *dare, pensare* and *credere* can all take a human or non human [à-object], as shown in the following sentences:

> *Ugo diede un libro a Maria*   (Ugo gave a book to Mary)
> *Ugo diede una spolverata alla credenza*   (Ugo gave the sideboard a wipe)
> *Ugo crede (a Maria + alla teoria)*   (Ugo believes in (Mary + the theory))
> *Ugo ha pensato (a Maria + alla teoria)*   (Ugo thought of (Mary + the theory))

The form of a pronoun corresponding to the [à-object] of one of these verbs is given in the table below[7]

---

[6] In fact, an Italian [subject] pronoun is erased when this erasing does not create any ambiguity. There is no room in this paper to discuss this complex phenomenon, which is also to be found in Spanish and Portuguese.

[7] The pronouns preceded by the preposition *a* are not placed before the verb.

TABLE 1	HUMAN			NON HUMAN		
	mas-sing	fem-sing	plural	mas-sing	fem-sing	plural
dare	gli	le	loro	gli	le	loro
credere	gli	le	loro	ci	ci	ci
pensare	a lui	a lei	a loro	ci	ci	ci

In Italian as well as in French, the form of an [à-object] pronoun can only be obtained by consulting a "lexicon-grammar" (M. Gross 1975, 1986 ; A. Elia et alii 1981). For each verb, a lexicon-grammar records all its syntactic properties, among them those concerning pronominalization.

5) The synthesis of the verb. In French, a [dir-object] of the third person singular is pronominalized as *le* if the previous occurrence of the token is masculine, as *la* if feminine :

*Ugo, je **le** vois souvent*   (Ugo, I often see him)

*Marie, je **la** vois souvent*   (Mary, I often see her)

However, if the first letter of the conjugated verb is a vowel, there is elision of *le* or *la* into *l'* :

*Ugo, je **l'**ai vu et je **l'**entends*   (Ugo, I saw him and I hear him)

*Marie, je **l'**ai vue et je **l'**entends*   (Mary, I saw her and I hear her)

This elision changes the computation of the morphological antecedents of the pronoun as shown in 4.2. Therefore, it has to be taken into account when determining if the [dir-object] has to be pronominalized. Other elisions of *Ppv* are to be found when the first letter of the conjugated verb is a vowel, for example the elision of *me* into *m'* :

*Ugo **me** voit et **m'**entend*   (Ugo sees me and hears me)

Contrary to the elision of *le* or *la* into *l'*, the elision of *me* into *m'* does not change the computation of the antecedents of the pronoun : *me* or *m'* can refer only to the speaker. Therefore, this elision can be one of the last operations performed by the generation system.

In Italian, the synthesis of the [dir-object] raises the same problems as it does in French, since there is elision of the pronouns *lo* and *la* into *l'* :

*Ugo, **l'**ho visto e lo sento*   (Ugo, I saw him and I hear him)

This elision is ruled by more complicated conditions than it is in French. It does not only depend upon the first letter of the conjugated verb being a vowel, as shown in the following examples :

Questo profumo, Ugo lo offre spesso a Maria   (This perfume, Ugo often offers it to Mary)

Questo profumo, Ugo l'offrirà domani a Maria(This perfume, Ugo will offer it tomorrow to Mary)

6) The synthesis of other complements. This factor involves several non local dependencies, among them the following ones for French[8] :

a) An [à-object] cannot be pronominalized as a *Ppv* if there is a [dir-object] synthesized as one of the following *Ppv* =: *me, te, nous, vous, se* :

> *Marie, je la présenterai à Ugo --> Je la lui présenterai*
> (Mary, I will introduce her to Ugo --> I will introduce her to him)
> *Toi, je te présenterai à Ugo --> * Je te lui présenterai*
> (You, I will introduce you to Ugo --> I will introduce you to him)

b) A [loc-object] designing a source locative cannot be pronominalized as the *PPv* =: *en* if there is a [dir-object] synthesized as the *Ppv* =: *en* :

> *Ces bonbons, je les ai sortis de la boîte --> Je les en ai sortis*
> (These candies, I pulled them out of the box --> I pulled them out of it)
> *Des bonbons, j'en ai sortis de la boîte --> * J'en en ai sortis*
> (Candies, I pulled some of them out of the box --> I pulled some of them out of it)

c) A [loc-object] designing a scenic locative cannot be pronominalized as the *PPv* =: *y* if there is a [à-object] synthesized as the *Ppv* =: *y* :

> *Marie, je l'ai rencontrée en Italie --> Je l'y ai rencontrée*
> (Mary, I met her in Italy --> I met her there)
> *Marie, j'y ai pensé en Italie --> * J'y y ai pensé*
> (Mary, I thought of her in Italy --> I thought of her there)

The non local dependencies described in a), b) and c) for French are observed in similar conditions for Italian. The following dependencies are observed only for Italian:

d) A [loc-object] designing a scenic locative cannot be pronominalized as the *Ppv* =: *ci* if there is a first person plural [dir-object] or [à-object] synthesized as the *Ppv* =: *ci* :

> *Ugo ti ha incontrato in Italia --> Ugo ti ci ha incontrato*
> (Ugo met you in Italy --> Ugo met you there)
> *Ugo ci ha incontrati in Italia --> * Ugo ci ci ha incontrati*
> (Ugo met us in Italy --> Ugo met us there)

---

[8] (M. Gross 1968) presents a complete list of dependencies between the French *Ppv*.

e) An [à-object] of the third person singular can be pronominalized as *gli* if the previous occurrence of the token is masculine, as *le* if feminine (see Table 1). However, if there is a [dir-object] or [de-object] synthesized as one of the following *Ppv* =*: lo, la, li, le, l', ne*, the pronouns *gli* or *le* amalgamate with this *Ppv* and both become *glie* :

> *Diedi il libro a Maria* --> *Le diedi il libro*
> (I gave the book to Mary --> I gave the book to her)
> *Diedi il libro a Ugo* --> *Gli diedi il libro*
> (I gave the book to Ugo --> I gave the book to him)
> *Il libro, lo diedi a (Maria + Ugo)* --> *Glielo diedi*
> (The book, I gave it to (Mary + Ugo) --> I gave it to her/him)

4.2 Computation of the morphologically compatible antecedents of the foreseen pronoun

A token, which does not refer to the speaker(s) or hearer(s), corresponds to a morphological antecedent of the foreseen pronoun if it has been previously synthesized as a nominal phrase the morphological features (i.e. gender and number) of which are compatible with the form of the foreseen pronoun. For example, if the foreseen pronoun is :
- the French [subject] pronoun *il* , its morphological antecedents are the masculine singular noun
- the Italian [à-object] pronoun *gli* , its morphological antecedents are the masculine singular noun phrases;
- the Italian [à-object] pronoun *le* , its morphological antecedents are the feminine singular noun phrases;
- the Italian [à-object] pronoun *glie* (result of an amalgamation of *gli* or *le* with another *Ppv*), its morphological antecedents are the singular noun phrases.

In the cases mentionned above, the computation of the morphological antecedents of the foreseen pronoun (i.e. the computation of the list L1) only depends upon the form of the pronoun. The computation of L1 may also depend upon the synthesis of other elements, thereby involving non local dependencies. For example, when the foreseen pronoun is *l'* (result of an elision of *le* or *la*), its morphological antecedents are all the singular noun phrases if the conjugated verb does not include a past participle as in *Je l'entends* (I hear him/her/it) ; otherwise, its morphological antecedents are the singular noun phrases with the gender indicated by the past participle. Recall that there is agreement in gender (and number) between a past participle and a pronominalized [dir-object]. In *Je l'ai vu* (I saw him/it), the morphological antecedents of *l'* are the masculine singular noun phrases, while in *Je l'ai vue* (I saw her/it), the morphological antecedents of *l'* are the feminine singular noun phrases. This is why the synthesis of the [dir-object] depends upon that of the verb (cf. 3.2). In fact, the synthesis of the [dir-object] also depends upon that of a possible attribute of the direct object, as shown below:
- in *Je l'estime beau* (I consider him/it beautiful) with the masculine adjective *beau* , the morphological antecedents of *l'* are the masculine singular noun phrases;

- in *Je l'estime belle* (I consider her/it beautiful) with the feminine adjective *belle* , the morphological antecedents of *l'* are the feminine singular noun phrases;
- in *Je l'estime fragile* (I consider him/her/it fragile) with the adjective *fragile* which is both masculine and feminine, the morphological antecedents of *l'* are all the singular noun phrases.

This implies that the inflected forms of adjectives, which is morphological information, has to be taken into account when determining if a token can be synthesized as a personal pronoun. Similar morphological considerations have to be taken into account for the erasing of an Italian [subject] pronoun, a matter that is not discussed here (see note 6).

4.3 Computation of the morphologically and syntactically compatible antecedents of the foreseen pronoun

The computation of the morphologically compatible antecedents of the foreseen pronoun returns a list L1 of tokens. Among those tokens, some may be syntactically incompatible with the envisionned pronoun. For example, in *Mary hated her,* the pronoun *her* cannot refer to *Mary* . The token representing *Mary* is said to be syntactically incompatible with the pronoun *her* . This coreferential syntactic incompatibility can be stated in the following rule:

> if a personal pronoun synthesizes a complement in a clause template, then it does not refer to the subject of this clause template, because if it did, it would be synthesized as a reflexive pronoun (* *Mary$_i$ hates Mary$_i$* --> *Mary$_i$ hates herself*) .

Another example of coreferential syntactic incompatibility can be stated in the following rule:

> if a pronoun synthesizes the subject of a sentential clause which must be reduced to an infinitive form when its subject is equal to the subject of the main clause, then this pronoun does not refer to the subject of the main clause, because if it did, the sentential clause would be reduced to an infinitive form (* *Mary$_i$ wants that Mary$_i$ leaves* --> *Mary$_i$ wants to leave*).

An illustration of this rule is that in *Mary wants that she leaves,* the pronoun *she* cannot refer to *Mary* .

4.4 Computation of the morphologically, syntactically and semantically compatible antecedents of the foreseen pronoun

The computation of the morphologically and syntactically compatible antecedents of the foreseen pronoun returns a list L2 of tokens. Among these tokens, some may be semantically incompatible with the envisionned pronoun. The first reason why a token can be semantically incompatible with the foreseen pronoun is associated with the human nature of the token. Go back to TABLE 1 that records the orm of an Italian [à-object] pronoun according to the verb and to the gender, number and human nature of the [à-object]. TABLE1 shows that:

the [à-object] pronoun *ci* , which appears with verbs such as *credere* or *dare* , can refer only to non human tokens. The human tokens are said to be semantically incompatible with the [à-object] pronoun *ci*.

the [à-object] pronoun *gli* can refer
> either to human or non human tokens when the verb behaves as *dare* ,
> or only to human tokens when the verb behaves as *credere* .

The second reason why a token can be semantically incompatible with the foreseen pronoun is associated with distributional constraints. An illustration of distributional constraints is the following one: the direct object of the verb *iron* in the active (its subject in the passive) must denote an item of clothing and not, for example, a piece of furniture. Therefore, in the discourse

The shirt is on the table. It was ironed recently .

he pronoun *it* refers compulsorily to *the book* and not to *the table* . The token representing *the table* is said to be semantically incompatible with the pronoun *it* .

4.5 Last decisions

The computation of the morphologically, syntactically and semantically compatible antecedents of the foreseen pronoun returns a list L3 of tokens.
At a rough estimate, if the number of elements of L3 is one, then the foreseen pronoun can be synthesized since it does not lead to ambiguity, whereas the foreseen pronoun should not be synthesized if the number of elements in L3 is greater than one since it would lead to ambiguity. Yet, it is well known that pragmatic and structure parallelism considerations may allow a pronoun to be non ambiguous even if L3 has more than one element (G. Hirst 1981, C. Sidner 1981, K. McKeown 1985, L. Danlos 1987a)[9]. Those considerations, which will not be discussed here, have to be taken into account to determine whether the foreseen pronoun has to be actually synthesized.

5 Other interactions of decisions with the pronominalization issue

We have shown in 4.1 and 4.2 that pronominalization involves the morphological level. Hence, the following result: the morphological level should be taken into account before the very last stage of the generation process.

---

[9] It may also happen that the foreseen pronoun should not be synthesized when the number of elements of L3 is one, because the distance between the antecedent and the pronoun is too great, for example.

In our generation model which is modularized into a strategic component and a syntactic component, the decisions made in the strategic component are independent from the pronominalization decisions which are all made in the syntactic component. We are going to show that this may be wrong.

First, let us point out that our generation model does not handle all the syntactic transformations in the same way: some transformations are decided in the strategic component, while other are decided in the syntactic component. For example, the passive transformation is decided in the strategic component since a discourse structure indicates if a sentence must be in the active or in the passive. This is justified by the fact that the choice between active and passive (with or without agent) is relevant to the discourse semantics (L. Danlos 1987a), as shown in the following pair of sentences:

John shot Mary who was killed.
Jon shot Mary whom he killed.

The first sentence, whose relative clause is in the passive without agent, expresses a causal relation between John's shooting and Mary's death. This is not the case for the second sentence whose relative clause is in the active. Similarly, the "ergative" transformation must be decided in the strategic component since it affects the discourse semantics, as shown in the following pair of sentences:

John knocked over the glass which broke.
John knocked over the glass which was broken.

The first sentence, whose relative clause is in the ergative, expresses a causal relation between the main clause and the relative clause. This is not the case for the second sentence, whose relative clause is in the passive without agent. Generally speaking, all the transformations that affect the discourse semantics should be decided "early", which means, in our generation model, in the strategic component.

On the other hand, the length permutation transformation and the dative transformation are decided in the syntactic component when placing the synthesized elements in the final clause. This is justified by the fact that these transformations can be decided only after the complements have been synthesized (cf. 3.3). Generally speaking, all the transformations that affect the sentence form and/or that depend upon the pronominalization decisions should be decided "late", which means, in our generation model, in the syntactic component.

Now, consider the clause templates that have a predicate as a subject, for example:

CL2   (:Cl (:subject PRED1) (:verb *plaire*) (à-object HUM2))

where the predicate PRED1 has the following definition:

```
PRED1 =: DRINK
AGENT = HUM1
OBJECT : wine
```

The token PRED1 can be synthesized as a pronoun if it has already been synthesized, like in the following discourse where the second sentence corresponds to the synthesis of Cl2:

Ugo boit du vin. Cela plaît à Marie   (Ugo drinks wine. It pleases Mary.)

If PRED1 is not synthesized as a personal pronoun, it is synthesized as a sentential clause:

(1) *Qu'Ugo boive du vin plaît à Marie*   (That Ugo drinks wine pleases Mary)

The form (1) is stylistically unpleasant, as it is the case for most forms with a sentential subject. One wants thus to avoid generating such forms. One way to improve (1) is by applying the subject extraposition transformation:

Il plaît à Marie qu'Ugo boive du vin   (It pleases Mary that Ugo drinks wine)

The decision to apply subject extraposition must be made after the pronominalization decisions, because subject extraposition cannot take place when the subject is pronominalized:

    Cela plaît à Ugo   (It pleases Ugo)
--> *Il plaît à Ugo cela*   (It pleases Ugo it)

Subject extraposition does not apply to any French verb (M. Gross 1975): roughly, it does not apply to transitive verbs:

(2) *Qu'Ugo boive du vin ravit Marie*   (That Ugo drinks wine delights Mary)
--> *Il ravit Marie qu'Ugo boive du vin*   (It delights Mary that Ugo drinks wine)

The form (2) is as stylistically unpleasant as (1), and thus should not be generated as such. One way to improve it is by applying the passive transformation:

Marie est ravie de ce qu'Ugo boive du vin (Mary is delighted by John drinking wine)

Hence, one would like to lay down the following rule:
    if a [subject] predicate is not synthesized as a personal pronoun, synthesize it as a sentential clause and apply subject extraposition if possible, if not apply the passive transformation.

Such a rule can take place only after the pronominalization decisions, so in the syntactic component in our model. However, we have seen that the passive transformation, which is relevant to the discourse semantics, should be decided in the strategic component. Hence a contradiction which shows that our modularization into only two components - a strategic component and a syntactic component, the latter handling pronominalization - is even too modular.

Conclusion

A French and Italian syntactic component covering the phenomena described in Sections 3 and 4 has been implemented in a procedural Common-Lisp program. An English syntactic component covering some of these phenomena has been implemented in a declarative formalism using functional descriptions (J.M. Lancel et alii 1988). Note that the cross dependencies and morphological interactions presented in these sections concern only the synthesis of personal pronouns, putting aside the synthesis of sentential clauses, subordinate clauses and coordinated clauses (L. Danlos 1987b). The reader can guess the complexity of a robust syntactic component for Romance languages.

We have not yet designed a generation algorithm that would cover the phenomena described in Section 5, that is a generation algorithm which would handle a total interaction between the conceptual, linguistic, syntactic and morphological levels. Nevertheless and at least, we hope to have underlined the linguistic complexity of text generation, a complexity which is still underestimated.

Bibliography

Danlos, L., 1985, *Génération automatique de textes en langues naturelles* , Masson, Paris.

Danlos, L., 1987a, *The linguistic basis of text generation* , Cambridge   University Press, Cambridge.

Danlos, L., 1987b, A French and English Syntactic Component for Generation, *Natural Language Generation: New results in Artificial Intelligence, Psychology and Linguistics* , Kempen G. ed, Dortrecht/Boston, Martinus Nijhoff Publishers.

Danlos, L., Namer, F., 1988, Morphology and cross dependencies in the synthesis of personal pronouns in Romance languages, *Proceedings of COLING-88*, Budapest.

Elia, A., Martinelli, M., D'Agostino, E., 1981, *Lessico e strutture sintattiche. Introduzione alla sintassi del verbo italiano* , Napoli Liguori, Napoli.

Gross, M., 1968, *Grammaire transformationnelle du français: syntaxe du verbe* , Larousse, Paris.

Gross, M., 1975, *Méthodes en syntaxe* , Hermann, Paris.

Gross, M., 1986, Lexicon-Grammar, The Representation of Compound Words, *in Proceedings of Coling'86, 11th International Conference on Computational Linguistics* , Bonn.

Hirst, G., 1981, Discourse oriented Anaphora resolution, *American Journal of Computational Linguistics* , vol. 7, no 2.

Lancel, J.M., Otani, M., Simonin, N., Danlos, L., 1988, Sentence Parsing and Generation with a Semantic Dictionary and a Lexicon-Grammar, *in Proceedings of Coling'88* , Budapest.

McKeown, K., 1985, *Text generation* , Cambridge University Press, Cambridge.

Reinhart, T., 1983, *Anaphora and semantic interpretation* , Croom Helm, London.

Sidner, C., 1981, Focusing for Interpretation of Pronouns, *American Journal of Computational Linguistics,* vol. 7, no 4.

THE USE OF FINITE AUTOMATA IN THE
LEXICAL REPRESENTATION OF NATURAL LANGUAGE

Maurice Gross

Université Paris 7

Laboratoire d'Automatique Documentaire et Linguistique [1]
Centre d'Etudes et de Recherches en Informatique Linguistique[2]

Finite automata are tools which are well adapted to the representation of phenomena observed at various levels of the description of natural languages.

There are numerous cases where an utterance (word, phrase or sentence) is subject to formal changes that leave invariant its essence, in general its meaning. These changes generate new utterances that all share features, they must then be grouped into families or equivalence classes. Some of these cases correspond to natural linguistic phenomena subject to rules, others, such as spelling, are more artificial. Handling all of them is essential for computer processing of texts.

Much emphasis has been put in the literature (both linguistic and computational) on the recursive linguistic phenomena that are not finite-state, hence promoting context-free or recursively enumerable grammars as the major models of language (N. Chomsky 1959). At this point, linguists seem to have forgotten that the bulk of known linguistic phenomena is indeed finite-state, in syntax as well as in phonology.

This statement can be made on the basis of the description of written French elaborated at the LADL-CERIL and not from isolated examples, the representativity of which is always a question. We study here typical cases of commonly encountered phenomena that have immediate implications for natural language recognition.

O. An elementary step of linguistic analysis

Computerized texts are processed in order to locate some information, for example, to determine a set of documents pertaining to this information or else in view of translating them. The first processing step then consists in recognizing words. The simple words of a text are rather well defined: strings of certain characters between consecutive separators[3]. But words undergo grammatical variations, it is thus necessary to reconstruct from the inflected forms of words found in texts the normal forms of words which constitute the dictionary entries (which can be roots or words). This activity, often called lemmatization, consists essentially in cutting off grammatical suffixes from occurrences of inflected forms and in checking compatibility between roots and suffixes. Since suffixes depend on word classes and often on individual words, a complete dictionary of the language has to be built in order to represent all and only the possible combinations of roots and suffixes.

We call the electronic dictionary of simple words, the dictionary of word entries (or roots) containing the grammatical codes that determine all and only the inflected forms together with their grammatical value(s). The dictionary should meet the following condition:

---

[1]. Unit 819 of the CNRS.
[2]. FIRTECH Industries de la langue française.
[3]. There are howewer difficulties in drawing a clear line between the set of computer characters that constitutes the alphabet of the text and the set of separators (cf. M. Silberztein 1988, present volume).

(T) Given a text and a recognition procedure of words that uses the electronic dictionary, all the simple words of the text should be recognized, that is, there should not be any failure of the dictionary look up process.

This ideal requirement should be corrected to take into account two important facts about texts:

- they contain mispelled words,
- they contain proper names, more generally arbitrary forms (symbols, numerical forms) that cannot be listed a priori in a dictionary.

Such a dictionary system is being built for French, it is called DELA (B. Courtois 1987), and presently contains about 65.000 entries which generate more than 500.000 inflected forms. The numerous gaps in ordinary (paper) dictionaries, that is, their fundamental inaptitude to meet the test (T), are being bridged progressively, and more information than the minimal grammatical features we mentioned is being introduced (M. Gross 1988). In particular, codes that systematize derivational processes are added. For example, from a verb such as *to abbreviate* one can derive two other verbs: *to reabbreviate* and *to disabbreviate*; from these verbs one can form the three adjectives: *abbreviatable, reabbreviatable, disabbreviatable*. These derivatives are missing in current dictionaries, but they must be entered in an electronic dictionary.

Listing such words alphabetically in a dictionary provides satisfactory computational solutions for retrieving them. But when one deals with such families of words, the regular syntactic and semantic relations that define them have to be recorded in view of processing operations that go beyond simple retrieval of the words. In our example, the semantic effect of affixation by *re-, dis-, -able* being general, the meaning relations between words (i.e. **repetition, suppression, potential**) that mirror the morphological relations could be used in formal procedures, hence should appear in the dictionary.

This example illustrates only one of the many reasons that lead us to entirely revise the notion of dictionary for the automatic treatment of texts and that force us to define precise representations for their entries.

1. Spelling

1.1 Spelling of simple words

In principle, the spelling of *simple* words is well standardized in most of the languages that use a Roman alphabet. It is a necessary condition to the existence of convenient dictionaries. However, many variations are allowed:

- for example the use of capital letters as variants of small case letters in certain contexts: inside English titles, for all words at the beginning of a sentence, etc.;
- in French, accents may be omitted from capital letters.

Thus a word such as *été* which means both "summer" and "been", is spelled either *Été* or *Eté* when it occurs at the beginning of a sentence. Hence the three possible spellings represented by the graph of figure 1.

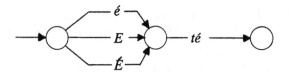

Figure 1

Notice that for other stylistic reasons (title, emphasis, etc.) words may have to be spelled entirely in capitals letters. Our example then has the two other spellings:

ETE, ÉTÉ

which can be incorporated into the preceding graph, yielding:

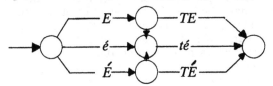

Figure 2

A recognition system for words must take into account the fact that there are 4 variants for the standard word form *été*[4]. Ignoring altogether differences in cases and accents renders equivalent all the forms of the graph of figure 2. As a matter of fact, early computer and communication systems have used this approximation. But from a linguistic and computational point of view, this solution is inadequate. In the particular example of *été*, using *ETE* as the canonical form for the equivalence class of spellings has no special implication for the recognition process of this word, but for the form *étés*, which only means "summers", using the canonical form *ETES* would introduce an artificial ambiguity with the verbal form of *être* (to be): *êtes* (are).

By transforming the electronic dictionary of French DELA and comparing the different versions, one can enumerate the artificial ambiguities generated by such approximations (S. Woznika 1987): The result is that more than 10 % of the inflected words, that is 50.000 words, become ambiguous[4].

A similar experiment has been performed by transforming the four "accents" of French (i.e. acute, grave, circumflex and umlaut) into one single diacritic sign: the "flat" accent. In this case, only a few dozen inflected words become ambiguous; for example, *prés* (meadows) and *près* (near), *pécher* (to sin) and *pêcher* (to fish); *dés* (dice) and *dès* (as soon) take on the same form *dès*, but no ambiguity with *des* (some) is generated as with the suppression of all accents. No ambiguity results for the words *êtes* and *étés*.

Whatever the practical solution adopted for recognizing words in texts representations such as those of figure 2 will have to be used, at least in the ambiguous cases.

Another type of spelling variants occurs with words which are not yet well established in the vocabulary of the language, this is the case for foreign imports or with slang words which begin acquiring respectability when exhibited in print. For example the word *kosher* can be found in French spelled at least in any of the following forms (M. Mathieu-Colas 1987):

---

[4]. In principle, other mixtures of cases are not found in the non technical vocabulary (cf. M. Silberztein 1987).

kasher, casher, kashère, cashère, kacher, kachère

They are all pronounced in the same way and it is clear that the variations are due to the various transcription solutions allowed by French. As a consequence, the forms can be organized in a graph in a natural way:

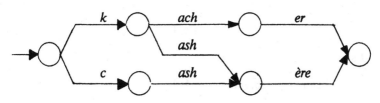

Figure 3

The shape of the graph avoids the combination of *ach* with the initial *c*, perhaps because of a potential ambiguity: *cacher* is a verb (to hide). In the same way one could easily add 6 variant forms with an *o* or *aw* instead of the *a*. With the same restriction on *c*, the modified graph of figure 3 would not introduce the two forms *cocher* (coachman) and *cochère* (about coach) which already exist, thus avoiding two ambiguities.

Remark.

The representations could be extended to spelling mistakes which are recognized as frequent or that can be expected sooner or later. For example, the spelling of *kasher* with *kh* instead of *c* or *k* is not found and would probably be considered as a mistake. One can expect to find it, given the already wide range of variations more or less accepted. This new possibility can be added to the graph of figure 3.

1.2 Spelling of compound words

While recording and spelling simple words is a well normalized activity, it is not the case for compound words in French. One reason could be the fact that compounds are not systematically entered into dictionaries. Since they are composed of at least two simple words, entering them together with one or the other simple component is an art that lexicographers practice with wide variations.

All the spelling problems mentioned for simple words also affect compounds. But new factors intervene. For example, in French, the use of hyphens in compound terms is not subject to rules. Consider the ways the compound noun *Middle Ages* is spelled in current French dictionnaries:

- it can be found with a hyphen or a space between the two simple words,
- it can be spelled with initial capitals or not.

Hence we find: *moyen(-)âge, Moyen(-)Age, Moyen(-)Âge, Moyen(-)âge*. These 8 forms are generated by the graph of figure 4:

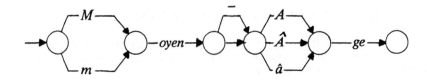

Figure 4

However, the 4 shapes:

$$moyen(-) \, Age, \, moyen(-) \, \widehat{A}ge$$

are not observed, either they should be substracted from the set generated by the graph, or else a different graph should be used as in figure 5:

Figure 5

Remark

Notice that the "missing" forms cannot be excluded by a general rule constraining the use of capital letters in compound nouns. In fact, the normal spelling of Pacific Ocean is with one capital on the second word: *océan Pacifique*.

Another source of variation for French compound words is the plural mark, in general an *-s* which is not pronounced. Hence, detecting its presence is a problem of syntactic analysis of the context, but often, this analysis fails to provide an answer. Consider for example the compound *un simulateur de vol* (a flight simulator), there is no phonetic, syntactic or semantic reason not to spell it *un simulateur de vols*. As a matter of fact, there are semantic rules (taught in school!) which determine the number of some compounds: for example *un essuie-mains* (a hand towel) is spelled with *mains* in the plural "because one usually dries both hands when one uses it".

In the same way, a *presse citron* (a lemon crusher) is spelled with *citron* in the singular, "because one crushes only one lemon at a time"[5]. This line of reasoning can lead to the spelling *vols*. However, the singular form is also observed and we thus have to represent the compound with an optional *-s* on *vol*[6].

---

[5]. Such "rules" never reflect reality, for example it is never the case that whole lemons are crushed, they are always cut in halves each of which is crushed.
[6]. Notice that the problem almost arises in English: *flight simulator* or *flights simulator* ? Since the second word begins with an *s*, the interdiction of the plural of *flight* may be hard to perceive. In the general case however, say with *baby boom*, it is clear that *babies boom* is not a possible variant.

2. Derivational morphology

As already mentioned, families of words related by prefixation and suffixation processes can be organized by means of a finite-state graph. Such a representation is particularly interesting in certain productive cases. We now study an example that presents a double productivity:

- nouns of countries or ethnical names range in the thousands. For example, the word *France* belongs to a set of proper nouns which can grow without any limit,
- such nouns give rise to a wide variety of derivatives. For example, we will see that at least 30 simple words can be formed on *France*. The two processes combine: namely each of the thousands of proper names enters derivational processes similar to those of *France* which we now examine.

Several subfamilies of such words are represented in figure 6:

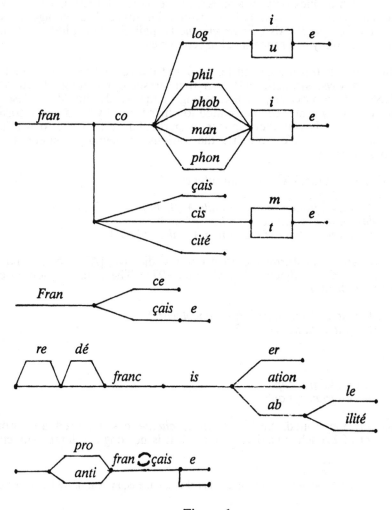

Figure 6

- a group of words formed on the form *franco-* with suffixes carrying obvious meanings,
- a group of words built only with suffixes on the root *fran* (in fact *franc*, but the two spellings *ç* and *c* of the sound *s* are separated);
- two words with capital F: *France* and *Français* (a Frenchman);
- a group of prefixed and suffixed words built on *-franc-is-*, that is a verbal derivative of the adjective *français*;
- a group of adjectives with prefixes *pro-* and *anti-* which can also be spelled as compounds, with a blank or a hyphen.

These graphs do not provide a complete representation of the forms of the family. There are in fact more simple words associated to the subgroup of the verb *franciser* (to make something French) which must be conjugated, yielding about 40 new forms; the noun *Français* (Frenchman or Frenchmen) and the adjective *français* both exist in the feminine and feminine plural. However, the noun *français* (French language) has no feminine form; also, the unmarked plural of this noun is semantically different from the plural of the noun *Français*. Moreover, the representation makes it difficult to introduce the prefixe *in-* which applies only to a subset of the words derived from the verb. For example, we have *inrefrançisable* (which cannot be made French again), whereas *inrefranciser* is not accepted[7]. Also, *Francophonie* is spelled with capital *F* (the meaning is roughly "the community of French speaking countries".

All the relations represented in figure 6 and the restrictions mentioned tend to mirror, but not always, syntactic relations that preserve meaning (J. Dubois 1962, D. Corbin 1988). More precisely, each meaning of the words should be described by means of an elementary sentence and related to other forms by formal transformations. Relations between words will then appear as particular restrictions to words of the syntactic transformations. We now list the various elementary sentences and the transformations involved.

There is a series of sentences with human subject:

	Max est un franco (mane + phile + phobe)
[NA] =	*Max est franco (mane + phile + phobe)*
[AN] =	*Max a une certaine franco (man + phil + phob)ie*

[NA], the first relation transforms the noun into an adjective; [AN], the second relation is a nominalization of the adjective (A. Meunier 1977). The following sentence is also obtained by nominalization:

	Max est un francologue (?un francologiste)
[NN] =	*Max fait de la francologie[8]*

We have as above:

	Max est un francophone
[NA] =	*Max est francophone*

As already mentioned, the noun *Francophonie* has acquired an autonomous meaning (the set of French speaking countries), it is no longer related syntactically to

---

[7]. For a detailed discussion, cf. M. Gross 1988.

[8]. These forms may sound odd to French speakers, but they are the equivalent of well accepted pairs such as:

	Max est sinologue
=	*Max fait de la sinologie*

the noun or to the adjective *francophone*, the relation is etymological. The verb *francophoniser* is used in Quebec, derivatives such as *infrancophonisable* or *francophonisation* follow mechanically.

The human noun *Français* is related to the human adjective by means of the general rule [NA]:

[NA] =
>*Max est un Français* (Max is a Frenchman)
>*Max est français* (Max is French)

(notice the use of capitals).

The non human adjective *français* (French) is to be distinguished from the human adjective of citizenship which has an identical form. It is this non human adjective that enters in relation with the causative verb *franciser*. We have then the following complex derivation (M. Gross 1981):

[Caus. *rendre*] =
[Caus. *-is*] =
>*(Ce mot + Ce produit) n'est pas français*
>*Max rend français (ce mot + ce produit)*
>*Max francise (ce mot + ce produit)*[9]

Then the verb *franciser* has variant forms generated by morpho-syntactic processes. The suffixes that appear in figure 5 correspond to syntactic relations such as:

[*pouvoir* i.] =
[Passive] =
[*Adj-able*] =
[*N-abilité*] =
>*On francise ce mot*
>*On peut franciser ce mot*
>*Ce mot peut être francisé*
>*Ce mot est francisable*
>*Ce mot a une certaine francisabilité*

[*N-ation*] =
[Passive] =
[*N-ation*] =
>*On a francisé ce mot*
>*On a fait la francisation de ce mot*
>*Ce mot a été francisé*
>*Ce mot a (eu + subi) une francisation*

[*être N-ation*] =
>*Coquetel est une francisation de cocktail*

One could also propose the relation:

[AN] =
>*Ce terme est un francisme* (This term is French-like)
>*Ce terme a une certaine francité*
>(This term belongs to the French domain)

Although syntactically motivated, this relation does not account for the meanings (sometimes unclear) of these word forms. It should be noted that we have dealt here with two different meanings of *francisation*, that is, two different words that cannot be clearly distinguished by morphological processes.

The prefixes *re-* and *dé-* apply here in a fairly regular way: *re-* can mean "again" and *dé-* indicates a "reverse" process. We mentioned the "negative" suffix *in-* which only applies to the three adjectival forms in *-able*, and thus cause the representation to be more complex. The relations involved are of the type:

---

[9]. Actually, the analysis should be more complex in order to account for the syntactic and semantic similarity between *franciser* and the operator verb *transformer* as observed in the pair:

>*Max a transformé ce mot étranger en un mot français*
>*Max a francisé cocktail en coquetel*

[re-V]	*Ce mot peut être refrancisé*
[Nég i.] =	*Ce mot ne peut pas être refrancisé*
[in-Adj-able] =	*Ce mot est inrefrancisable*
[AN] =	*Ce mot n'a aucune refrancisabilité*

The proper human noun Français (*Frenchman*) is related to *France* and to the human adjective *français* (French). One of the reasons for isolating this noun-adjective pair is its property of accepting the prefixes *pro* and *anti* which are not accepted with the other meaning (i.e. with non human subjects). Underlying this prefixation are the syntactic relations:

(Bob + ce livre) est (contre + pour) (la France + les Français)
= *(Bob + ce livre) est (anti + pro)français*
(Bob + this book) is (against + for) (France + the French)

It should be noted that the rules used so far in our relations involve support or operator verbs (e.g. *être, avoir, pouvoir, rendre*), that is, grammatical verbs with limited semantic function (e.g. modality, causative). Hence, the syntactic relations we presented do not make meaning explicit. In certain cases, we may need to make the relations more specific by introducing elementary sentences which contain verbs that carry complete meanings. Z.S. Harris 1976 has proposed such a device as an explanation of the meaning, and at any rate, as an etymological possibility. For example, one could introduce pairs such as the following, in order to complement the syntactic derivations given above:

Bob étudie la France (Bob studies France)
= *Bob est un francologue* (= Bob is a francologist)

Bob (aime + hait) la France (Bob (loves + hates) France)
= *Bob est franco(phile + phobe)* (= Bob is franco(phile + phobe))

La France obsède Bob (France obsesses Bob)
= *Bob est francomane* (= Bob is francomaniac)

Bob parle le français (Bob speaks French)
= *Bob est francophone* [10] (= Bob is francophone)

Bob étudie le français (Bob studies French)
= *Bob est un franciste* (= Bob is a specialist of French)

These semantic relations involve explicit sentences which could be used as semantic representations for the equivalence classes of sentences generated by the syntactic transformations. These representations are summed up in the table of Figure 7.

---

[10]. This nominal sentence is more specific than the verbal one, from an aspectual point of view: there is a permanent component in the fact that Bob speaks French.

Derived words	Semantic predicates	Basic words
francologue	**étudier**	*la France*
francomane	**obsédé par**	*la France*
francophile	**aimer**	*la France*
francophobe	**détester**	*la France*
francophone	**parler**	*le français*
franciste	**étudier**	*le français*
franciser	**rendre comme**	*français*

Two words of the third column are linked by a relation such as: *Le français se parle en France* (French is spoken in France).

Figure 7

One of the reasons for structuring this set of words is its productivity. Hundreds of other names of place can enter the same type of graph. However every such graph will have to be constructed "manually", mechanical substitution of roots would run into difficulties due to numerous idiosyncrasies. For example, the correspondance between country names and language names or between countries names and citizen names is not one-to-one. There are social or political groups other than countries, their names give rise to similar families, with gaps (e.g. no language name). Morphology can be fairly regular with differences such as in the pairs: *English-anglo, American-americano*. But they can also be highly irregular. Already, pairs such as *Fran(ce + çais)-franco*, where the reason for the sound /k/ in *co* is not clear, are not uncommon: *Belgique-belgo* raises a similar question for the sound /g/ in *go*. And often, some forms are unrelated in shape to the intended root: there are series such as:

$$\left\{ \begin{array}{lll} \textit{Allemagne (N),} & \textit{allemand (N, Adj), germanique (Adj),} & \textit{germano} \\ \textit{Espagne (N),} & \textit{espagnol (N, Adj), hispanique (Adj),} & \textit{hispano} \\ \textit{Suisse (N),} & \textit{suisse (N, Adj), helvétique (Adj),} & \textit{hélvéto} \end{array} \right.$$

Such forms are often complementary, in the sense that if we wanted to construct for *Germany* the dictionary article we elaborated for *France*, we would have to replace the words constructed on *fran* by words constructed sometimes on *alleman*, sometimes on *german*, sometimes on both (e.g. *germanophile, *allemanophile*, whereas *études allemandes* and *études germaniques* are both accepted and mean both German studies).

There are other families of compounds that raise similar problems, for example, scientific terms in the fields of physics, chemistry, biology, medicine, etc.

An interesting situation arises with all these families of words when they are composed in the following way: forms ending with *-o* can be considered as adverbs which modify adjectives derived from place, ethnic or field names. For example, we obtain compound adjectives as the product of the set of adverbial prefixes by the set of adjectives of nationality:

$$(P) \left\{ \begin{array}{ll} \textit{anglo} & \textit{anglais} \\ \textit{franco} & \textit{français} \\ \textit{germano} & \textit{allemand, germanique} \\ \textit{hispano} & \textit{espagnol, hispanique} \\ \textit{luso} & \textit{portugais, lusitanien} \end{array} \right.$$

The interpretation of the compounds is that of conjunctions, with variations that depend on the noun to which the combination is attached:

- *un mélange franco-anglais* is a mixture of French and English stuff,
- *un accord franco-anglais* is an agreement between France and England (Great Britain),
- *la frontière franco-anglaise* would be the boundary between France and England.

Products such as (P) can in principle be generalized[11] to any length, as in:

   un accord anglo-americano-allemand

the general shape would then be:

(Q)   **(anglo)^n-(anglais)**

representable by a finite automaton. The number of elements that can be substituted in the parentheses may not be finite.

In the same way, a productive family of adverbs is of the form:

   à la (française + anglaise + italienne + etc.)

They can be analyzed as a reduction of the adverbs:

   à la manière (française + anglaise + italienne + etc.)

where the N =: *manière* (manner, way) makes their meaning more explicit (i.e. *in the French way*).

The representation we outlined is far from complete, for there are many combinations frozen to various degrees involving the simple words *France*, *français*, etc. which have lost their original syntactic relations to these words. This is the case for example in *Revolution française* which has acquired a meaning of its own, *Banque de France*, the province *Ile de France* (and the derivative *ilofrancien*: inhabitant of this province), the city *Fort de France*, etc. Examples such as *études françaises* (French studies), *marine française,* (French Navy) seem different: on the one hand, the feeling is that one is dealing with compositional phrases, since productive syntactic patterns appear to hold:

   études sur la France = études françaises
   marine de la France = marine française, etc.

On the other hand, these relations do not preserve meaning exactly (i.e. the "institutional" character of the compound *NAdj* is not perceived in the source term.

3. Syntax

Similar problems of representation are raised by many combinations of words into sentences, solutions similar to those we applied to characters and parts of words can be used. The description of sentences then provides clear situations about the computational function of automata representations. We now present several cases of such formal descriptions.

---

[11]. Also, similar products exist, with different types of interpretation and combinatorial restrictions for other large parts of the vocabulary (e.g. socio-economic, cardio-vascular).

3.1 The grammar of French pre-verbal particles.

This example is a case of a strictly grammatical automaton, that is, a device enumerating a family of elementary sentences which have no meaning relations to each other. The automaton aims at generating all and only the sentences that contain non empty sequences of distinguished words, called pre-verbal particles (Ppv), also known as clitics, conjoined pronouns, etc. It should be noted that the justification for building a local grammar is linguistic in a specific way: the distinction between Ppvs and other pronouns is being formalized. When one studies sentences such as:

Elle ne le lui donne pas
(*She does not give it to him*)

one observes that no insertion is allowed in the sequences $(Ppv)^n V$ (V is the verb; the symbol * signals ungrammaticality):

*Elle souvent ne lui en donne pas
*Elle ne souvent ne lui en donne pas
*Elle ne lui en souvent donne pas

whereas in English for example, similar insertions are accepted:

She often gives some to him

French thus presents a phenomenon of pronominalization of complements that has drawn the attention of linguists because of its complexity. For example, the sentence form with two complements. (N_1 and $à N_2$):

$N_0 V N_1 à N_2$ =: *Max montre ce lit à Luc*
(Max is showing this bed to Luke).

leads to pronominal forms such as:

Max le montre à Luc
Max lui montre ce lit
Max le lui montre

where, in appropriate contexts, complements have been replaced by pre-verbal pronouns. The arrangement of pronouns is complex, for example, if the direct object is indefinite, its pronoun (*en*) occupies a different position, as in:

Max lui en montre un
(Max is showing one to him)

Subject pronouns have to be included in the description. They introduce other restrictions linked to the grammatical features of the subject and of the complements. The number of complements that are sources of Ppvs is limited and verbs take at most three or four complements that are sources of Ppvs. Even if we add subject pronouns and the negative particles *ne* to the set of Ppvs, the combinatorial problem remains finite and even relatively small. It is quite natural to represent all and only the sequences of Ppvs by means of a finite automaton. The combinations of Ppvs have been represented on the condensed graph of figure 8. For reasons of convenience, the notations differ slightly from those of the preceding finite automata, but their formal equivalence should be obvious. D. Perrin 1989 has discussed for such graphs various processes of representation that are better suited to computer treatment.

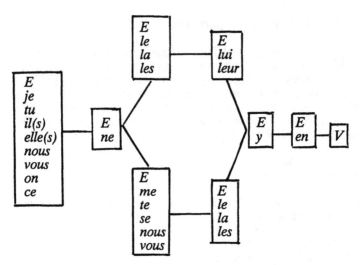

The symbol E represents the empty word. This graph does not take into account elision nor agreement phenomena of reflexive verbs.

Figure 8

The graph of figure 8 is incomplete because of elisions that may occur when some of the *Ppv*s come into contact. For example, the particle *ne* changes its form to *n'* when followed by a vowel. The vowel can belong to another *Ppv* as in *n'en*, *n'y* or to the verb, as in *n'arrive pas*. Such constraints are strictly finite and could be incorporated in the finite automaton of figure 8, making it more complex. However, this elision phenomenon occurs in more general contexts than combinations of *Ppv*s. It is observed with articles, (*le*, *la*), prepositions (*de*), conjunctions (*que*) in combination with practically any word beginning with a vowel v. The rule accounting for this contraction can be written:

$$\# (n + m + t + s + l + d + qu)e \# vx$$
$$= \# (n + m + t + s + l + d + qu)' vx$$

where the symbol $\#$ represents a blank. In other words, this formula can be seen as a transduction of sequences of characters. This transducer applies to the output of the automata of figure 8 providing all and only the correct sequences, and it may apply to many other syntactic forms.

Many independent linguistic phenomena interfere in general ways, they impose solutions by composition of automata. For example, so-called reflexive verbs (e.g. *se souvenir*) impose identity of person and number between the subject and an intrinsic *Ppv* which behaves exactly as a *Ppv* with an overt complement source:

> je me souviens de cela, je m'en souviens (I remember it)
> tu te souviens de cela, tu t'en souviens
> elle se souvient de cela, elle s'en souvient

> *je (te + se + nous + vous) en souviens
> *elle (me + te + nous + vous) en souvient, etc.

Reflexivization depends on particular verbs such as *se souvenir* (*Vrflx*) which may have other *Ppv*s not involved in the process (e.g. *en* in the above examples). With other verbs, the process involves two complements:

*Elle se montre à Bob,   *Elle se lui montre*

It is possible to represent all possibilities by graphs of the type of figure 8, however, a rule (i.e. a transduction) is sometimes more appropriate. For example, the agreement rule could apply to the string schema:

Ppv $(E + ne)$ **Ppv** $(Ppv)^k$ *Vrflx*

when the first *Ppv* is the subject, optionally followed by the negative particle *ne*, followed by the *Ppv* which must agree in gender and number with the subject, followed by k ($= 0$, *1, 2*) other *Ppv*s.

Let us now mention an application of this description of *Ppv*s to the automatic resolution of an ambiguity mentioned in 1, one of the systematic ambiguities generated by the suppression of accents. This ambiguity is seen in MANGES for example, which corresponds to both forms: 2nd person singular of the present tense: *manges* (eat) and masculine past participle: *mangés* (eaten). All transitive verbs of the first conjugation group, that is several thousands of verbs including most productive classes, have this ambiguity. However, the conjugated form *manges* necessarily implies the presence of the *Ppv* subject *tu* in its immediate context, namely:

- the interrogative form *manges-tu*, or
- the subgraph of figure 8 restricted to the subject *Ppv tu*.

Hence, mechanical disambiguation can be performed for shapes such as *MANGES* whose indeterminacy is detected by a dictionary look-up procedure: if the form has *tu* in its context, it is the finite verb, if *tu* is not found, it must be the participle form with accent.[12]

3.2 Frozen sentences

Another situation where finite automata find a general application is the description of elementary sentences which have frozen (idiomatic) parts such as:

$$Bob \; a \begin{pmatrix} nourri \\ réchauffé \end{pmatrix} \begin{pmatrix} un \; serpent \\ une \; vipère \end{pmatrix} \begin{pmatrix} sur \\ dans \\ en \end{pmatrix} son \; sein$$

(1) $$Bob \begin{pmatrix} nursed \\ nourished \\ warmed \\ cherished \end{pmatrix} \begin{pmatrix} a \; serpent \\ a \; snake \\ viper \end{pmatrix} \quad in \quad his \; bosom$$

The subject, a human noun, is free, in other words it has a wide range of variations, but the other terms of the sentences are entirely constrained in English as in French. These sets of sentences (12 for French, 12 for English) are naturally organized by a finite automaton which then represents the meaning common to all variant shapes.

Other variations can be either included in the basic automata or introduced by finite transductions of the basic forms. For example, the dependency (identity of person-number) between the possessive adjective, and the subject is finite, in the sense that it holds between the two positions N_0 and N_2 of a finite structure of the form $N_0 \, V \, N_1 \, Prep \, N_2$. A transducer which would apply in many other similar situations could represent this agreement constraint:

You warmed a serpent in your bosom

---

[12]. Except, when additional ambiguities occur accidentally.

You warmed a serpent in his bosom

It is the limitation on the number of basic complements (never more than three) that makes sentence patterns strictly finite.

More varied forms of sentences are obtained when the syntactic positions where the frozen parts occur are varied. For example, the two sentences:

(2)   *(God, The Lord) recalled Bob to Him*

both mean *Bob died*. They also have the form $N_0 V N_1 Prep N_2$ with N_0 and N_2 frozen[13], N_0 was free and N_1, N_2 frozen in example (1). The application of the [Passive] rule to (2) can be seen as a finite transduction of the structure $N_0 V N_1 Prep N_2$, which yields:

(3)   *Bob was recalled to (God, the Lord)*

Example (1) may also undergo [Passive], as in:

(4)   *Max is a serpent which was nursed in Bob's bosom*

(3) and (4) share a special feature of [Passive]: the pronominal elements (*his*, *him*) must be replaced by their full forms. Hence, two similar but not entirely identical transductions will have to apply to (1) and (2). Such differences are typical, they constitute one source of the enormous variety of syntactic forms allowable for a given meaning unit. Other formal changes come from the various adjunction processes (adverbs, relative clauses, noun complements, etc.). But in most cases, these adjunctions and the changes of word order can be described by composing finite transducers on strings of words or of grammatical categories.

3.3 Other forms

Many local grammars of phenomena that are stictly finite as in the case of French *Ppv*s have to be written. Some examples such as grammars of numerals (integers, fractions, decimal numbers) are well known. But often, they cannot be directly included in more complex grammars that describe numerical data: prices, lengths, weights, time, etc. The reason is that the particular units of price, length, weight, time, etc. constrain the numerals attached to them (e.g. hours in a day are only twenty four). Hence, specific grammars must be written in each situation[14], more precisely, specific composition operations of automata will have to be defined in each situation.

4. Conclusion

We have attempted to show that finite automata can adequately represent certain formal variations of linguistic units (from words to sentences). A number of questions arise immediately about any actual programme of description of a given language.

There are **linguistic questions**, such as:

- separating the meanings of each word, that is establishing a catalogue of ambiguities to be solved;
- describing the formal (i.e. morphosyntactic) variations possible for each word meaning;
- establishing reasonably complete lists of simple words and of processes of word formation;

---

[13]. A person-number agreement constraint may also hold between N_0 and N_2, but need not be represented since these two components cannot vary.
[14]. D. Maurel 1987, has written for french a detailed grammar of dates.

- establishing reasonably complete lists of compound words, including lists of elementary sentences whose variations are the object of a lexicon-grammar (M. Gross 1975; J.-P. Boons, A. Guillet, Ch. Leclère 1976).

All these questions are not independent. Thus a complete research programme must be defined to construct the linguistic system which will bear on the general vocabulary and on specialized vocabularies which may have their own linguistic properties. Without this complex device no significant picture of the language and no application can emerge.

There are also **computational questions** to be solved, such as:

- the choice of representations for families of strings. These representations will have to be implemented in computer programs;
- implementation of dictionaries of automata. These automata will be the basis of powerful look up procedures that attach to a particular word form general information invariant with respect to the family of strings defined by the automata;
- implementation of computer tools for constructing the dictionaries of automata, which includes maintenance tools for editing automata (adjunctions and suppressions of paths and word forms.

The experience we gained from the description of French indicates that many of these questions are still difficult to solve, even though the methods and the technology are available. Some of the questions we listed may look like problems already dealt with by specialists, they are in fact entirely new in most cases:

- traditional dictionaries are all phototypeset, that is available in computer form, nonetheless they are of limited use when an electronic dictionary has to be built,
- in the same way, traditional studies in morphology, namely in word formation, have never been pushed to the point where they could lead to automata representation, much less to dictionaries of automata,
- interesting software sometimes similar to that needed here already exists. But relational data bases, "tree editors" and automata systems such as the one H.Johnson and R. Kazman 1986 have developed for the Oxford English Dictionary do not seem specific enough to meet the demands an electronic dictionary puts on computer systems.

Many linguistic questions are language dependent, but formal and computer systems could be made general enough to be common to at least the main European languages. A coordinated effort of construction appears both necessary and feasible.

References

Boons, Jean-Paul, Alain Guillet, Christian Leclère 1976. *La structure des phrases simples en français, I. Constructions intransitives*, Genève : Droz, 377 p.

Chomsky, Noam 1956. Three Models for the Description of Language, *IRE Transactions on Information Theory*, IT2, pp. 113-114.

Corbin, Danièle 1988. *Morphologie dérivationnelle et structuration du lexique*, Thèse de Doctorat: Université Paris 7.

Courtois, Blandine 1987. *Le système DELA de dictionnaire électronique du français*, Rapport de recherches du LADL, Université Paris 7.

Dubois, Jean 1962. *Etudes sur la dérivation suffixale en français moderne et contemporain*, Paris : Larousse, 118 p.

Gross, Maurice 1975. *Méthodes en syntaxe*, Paris: Hermann, 414 p.

Gross, Maurice 1981. Les bases empiriques de la notion de prédicat sémantique, in *Langages*, N° 63, A. Guillet et C. Leclère éds. : *Formes syntaxiques et prédicats sémantiques*, pp. 7-52.

Gross, Maurice 1988. Sur la structure des articles d'un lexique-grammaire, *Linguistica Computazionale*, Pise.

Gross, Maurice 1989. La construction de dictionnaires électroniques du français, *Annales des Télécommunications*, Paris: CNET.

Harris, Zellig 1976. *Notes du cours de syntaxe*, Paris : Le Seuil, 237 p.

Kazman, Robert 1986. *Structuring the Text of the Oxford English Dictionary through Finite State Transductions*, University of Waterloo, Waterloo, Ontario: Internal Report CS-86.20.

Mathieu-Colas, Michel 1987. Variations graphiques de mots composés, *Rapport N° 4 du Programme de Recherches Coordonnées Informatique Linguistique*, Université Paris 7: LADL.

Maurel, Denis 1987. Grammaire des dates, *Mémoires du CERIL*, Vol. 1, CNAM et Université Paris 7, Paris : CERIL, pp.218-240.

Meunier, Annie 1977. Sur les bases syntaxiques de la morphologie dérivationnelle, *Lingvisticae Investigationes*, J. Benjamins B.V., Philadelphia-Amsterdam, pp. 287-332.

Perrin, Dominique 1989. Automates et algorithmes sur les mots, *Annales des Télécommunications*, Paris: CNET.

Silberztein, Max 1987. L'inversion de textes, *Rapport de recherche du Programme de recherches coordonnées Informatique Linguistique*, Paris: Université Paris 7: LADL.

Silberztein, Max 1988. The Lexical Analysis of French, present volume.

Woznika, Stanislas 1987. *Dictionnaire des homographes du français*, Rapport de recherches du LADL, Université Paris 7.

Estimation of the entropy by the Lempel-Ziv   method

G. Hansel

Université de Rouen/Mathématiques
BP 67
F-76130 Mont Saint-Aignan

Introduction

uppose that we observe a possibly infinite stochastic sequence of 0's

nd 1's appearing independently with probabilities α and β

espectively. The definition of the "entropy" of such a process goes

ack to the basic papers of C. Shannon [4] and is given by the formula

$$h = \alpha\log(1/\alpha)+\beta\log(1/\beta)$$

f we do'nt know the values of α and β and if we want to estimate the

alue of h, the simplest way is to observe a "long enough" sequence

roduced by the process, then to estimate α and β by the respective

requencies of 0's and 1's in the sequence and finally to apply the

bove formula.

ore precisely let $(a_n)_{n\in\mathbb{N}}$ be a sequence of 0's and 1's produced by

he process and for all $n \in \mathbb{N}$, let $f_n(0)$ and $f_n(1)$ be the frequencies of

and 1 in the finite sequence $a_1 \ldots a_n$ and let us define

$$h_n = f_n(0)\log(1/f_n(0)) + f_n(1)\log(1/f_n(1))$$

hen for almost every sequence produced by the process (that is to say

ith a probability 1) we have $h = \lim_n h_n$

e can even say more: some classical theorems, the laws of large

umbers, allow us to compute what is the size of a "long enough"

equence to get an estimation which has a given precision with less

han a given probability to be wrong.

If the initial process is not independent but is of a markovian type, a similar method can still be used. Suppose that the process is ruled by a transition matrix P= (p_{ij}), p_{ij} being the conditional probability to observe the state j after having observed the state i (here i and j are 0 or 1). The entropy of such a process is then given by the formula

$$h = \sum_{i,j} p_i p_{ij} \log(1/p_{ij})$$

the numbers p_i being the probability measures of the different states of the process. Again, we can estimate the numbers p_i and p_{ij} by computing the adequate frequencies in a "long enough" sequence of observations and this gives us an estimation of h which converges to h almost surely . Also in this case classical theorems tell us what is "long enough" to achieve a given precision in the estimation of h.

Suppose now that our knowledge about the process is more reduced: we know only that the process is ruled by an invariant ergodic probabilty measure. In this case the situation is quite different. Let A = {0,1} and let us note $\mu(u) = \mu(a_1 a_2 \dots a_m)$ the probability to observe the sequence u = $a_1 a_2 \dots a_m \in A^m$. The entropy of the process is defined by the formula

$$h = \lim_m -\frac{1}{m} \sum_{u \in A^m} \mu(u) \log(\frac{1}{\mu(u)})$$

The process being ergodic, the number $\mu(u)$ is equal to the frequency of the word u in almost all infinite sequences produced by the process. So we could imagine to use the following method: 1) to fix a "large number m"; 2) to observe a "long enough sequence" produced by the process; 3) to estimate the numbers $\mu(u)$, $u \in A^m$, by the frequencies of the words u, $u \in A^m$, in the observed sequence and finally to get an estimation of h making use of the above formula. But this method is not good because we do'nt know what means "a large number m". The difficulty stems from the fact that we "must go twice to the infinity": if we note $f_n(u)$ the frequency of the word u in the sequence $a_1a_2...a_n$ we have

$$h = \lim_m \lim_n \sum_{u \in A^m} \lim_n f_n(u)\log(1/f_n(u))$$

In particular, for each fixed m, there exist ergodic processes such that the method will give a bad estimation of h.

So we can ask: does there exist an other method to estimate the entropy such that the estimations converge to the "true" number h for every ergodic process? More precisely we have to define a sequence of mappings $h_n : A^n \rightarrow \mathbb{R}$, $n \in \mathbb{N}$, such that for every ergodic process and for almost every sequence $(a_n)_{n \in \mathbb{N}}$ produced by the process

$$\lim_n h_n(a_1a_2...a_n) = h$$

A solution to this problem can be given by making use of a work of Ziv and Lempel [5] on text compression. For every finite or infinite sequence (a_n), they define a factorization in a sequence (w_n) of words on the alphabet A. Noting $|w|$ the length of the word w, if we put $n(k) = \sum_{i=1}^{k} |w_i|$, it turns out that for almost every sequence $(a_n)_{n \in \mathbb{N}}$ we have $\lim_{k \to \infty} \frac{k\log k}{n(k)} = h$ and this result leads immediately to a method of estimation satisfying to the desired conditions.

From the initial work of Lempel and Ziv, it results in a fairly indirect way that the above convergence is true in probability. The result for the almost sure convergence is certainly known by several persons but was never published. We give here a proof of it. A part of the proof (see section 5) is due to Gabriel [2].

2.Preliminaries

2.1.Definitions - Notations

Let A be a finite alphabet, A^* the set of all the finite sequences of elements of A (the *words*) endowed with the usual product, $A^{\mathbb{Z}}$ the set of all the bi-infinite sequences $(a_n)_{n \in \mathbb{Z}}$ of elements of A, $\sigma: A^{\mathbb{Z}} \to A^{\mathbb{Z}}$ the *shift* defined by $\sigma((a_n)_{n \in \mathbb{Z}}) = (a_{n+1})_{n \in \mathbb{Z}}$.

Let $u = b_1 b_2 \ldots b_n \in A^*$ be a word; we note $|u| = n$ the length of u and we associate to u the *cylinder*

$$[u] = \{ (a_n)_{n \in \mathbb{Z}} \in A^{\mathbb{Z}} / a_i = b_i, \ i = 1, \ldots, n \}.$$

Endowed with the product topology, $A^{\mathbb{Z}}$ is a compact space and the shift σ is a homeomorphism. Let $\mathcal{B}$ be the Borel σ-algebra of $A^{\mathbb{Z}}$. In the sequel μ denotes an invariant ergodic probability measure on $\mathcal{B}$, that is to say a mapping $\mu: \mathcal{B} \to [0,1]$ satisfying the conditions

1) for all $B \in \mathcal{B}$, $\mu(\sigma^{-1}(B)) = \mu(B)$ (invariance)

2) if $B \in \mathcal{B}$ satisfies $\sigma^{-1}(B) = B$, then $\mu(B) = 0$ or 1   (ergodicity).

The probability measure μ is completely determined by its value on the cylinders and in the sequel we note $\mu(u)$ instead of $\mu([u])$.

We observe that if B is a set of words with the same length, we can identify B with union B'of the associated cylinders and we note

$$\mu(B) = \sum_{u \in B} \mu(u)$$

In particular for all $m \in \mathbb{N}$, we have $\mu(A^m) = 1$.

The *entropy* $h = h(\mu)$ of the probability measure μ is the number

$$h = \lim_n -\frac{1}{n} \sum_{u \in A^n} \mu(u) \log(1/\mu(u))$$

In this definition "log" means the neperian logarithm. But in the proofs of the results which follow, the basis of the logarithms does'nt matter. So, to simplify the computations, we suppose that card(A) = 2 and that the basis of the logarithm is 2.

2.2. The Ziv's factorization

Let $\alpha = (a_n)_{n\in\mathbb{N}}$ be a sequence of elements of A. We define the *Ziv's factorization* of α as being the sequence $(w_n)_{n\in\mathbb{N}} = (w_n(\alpha))_{n\in\mathbb{N}}$ of words inductively defined by the conditions

$w_0 = a_0$;

$w_0, w_1, \ldots, w_k$ having been defined, if $w_0 w_1 \cdots w_k = a_0 a_1 \cdots a_n$, then $w_{k+1} = a_{n+1} a_{n+2} \cdots a_{n+m}$, where m is the least integer such that $a_{n+1} a_{n+2} \cdots a_{n+m} \notin \{w_0, w_1, \ldots, w_k\}$. For all $\alpha \in A^{\mathbb{N}}$ and all $k \in \mathbb{N}$ we note

$$n(k,\alpha) = |w_1(\alpha) w_2(\alpha) \ldots w_k(\alpha)| = \sum_{i=1}^{k} |w_i(\alpha)|$$

The purpose of what follows is to prove the

<u>Theorem</u> 1   Let μ be an invariant ergodic probability measure on $A^{\mathbb{Z}}$ and let h be the entropy of μ.

Then for μ-almost-every sequence $\alpha = (a_n)_{n\in\mathbb{Z}}$, $\lim\limits_{k\to\infty} \dfrac{k\log k}{n(k,\alpha)} = h$.

3. Some classical results [1][3]

In this section we collect some classical results from the ergodic theory which we shall use in the sequel.

Let $u = a_1 a_2 \ldots a_n \in A^*$ and let C be a set of words having the same length l, with $l \leq n$. The *frequency of C in u*, noted $f_C(u)$ is the number

$$f_C(u) = \frac{1}{n} \, \text{card}\{ \, i \in \{1, 2, \ldots, n-l+1\} \, / \, a_i a_{i+1} \cdots a_{i+l-1} \in C \, \}$$

Proposition 1 Let μ be an invariant ergodic probability measure on $A^{\mathbb{Z}}$;

1) For μ-almost-every sequence $(a_n)_{n \in \mathbb{Z}} \in A^{\mathbb{Z}}$, for all $1 \in \mathbb{N}$, and for every set C of words having the same length 1

$$\lim_n f_C(a_1 a_2 \ldots a_n) = \mu(C)$$

2) For every $\varepsilon > 0$, there exist a measurable set $B \in \mathcal{B}$ and an integer $n_0 \in \mathbb{N}$ such that

i) $\mu(B) > 1 - \varepsilon$

ii) for all $n \geq n_0$ and all $\alpha = (a_n)_{n \in \mathbb{Z}} \in B$

$$\frac{1}{2^{n(h+\varepsilon)}} \leq \mu(a_1 a_2 \ldots a_n) \leq \frac{1}{2^{n(h-\varepsilon)}}$$

Remark We shall also use in the sequel the following weaker form of the part 2) above

For all $\varepsilon > 0$, there exists $n_0 \in \mathbb{N}$ such that for every $n \geq n_0$, there exists a set C of words having the same length n and satisfying the conditions

i) $\mu(C) \geq 1 - \varepsilon$

ii) $\mathrm{card}(C) \leq 2^{n(h+\varepsilon)}$

4. Minorizing the entropy

In this section we fix a sequence $\alpha = (a_n)_{n \in \mathbb{N}}$ satisfying the condition (c0): for every set C of words which have the same length

$$\lim_n f_C(a_1 a_2 \ldots a_n) = \mu(C)$$

(recall that α exists by proposition 1). We note $n(k)$ instead of $n(k, \alpha)$. We are going to prove some properties of the Ziv's factorization of the sequence α.

Let ε be fixed and let $\varepsilon' \ll \varepsilon$; the exact requirements satisfied by ε' will be completed later.

By the weak form of the proposition 1 , there exist an integer l and a set C of words of length l satisfying the conditions

(c1) $l > 1/\varepsilon'$

(c2) $\mu(C) > 1-\varepsilon'$

(c3) $\text{card}(C) < 2^{l(h+\varepsilon')}$

For all $k \in \mathbb{N}^*$, let us note $W_k = \{ w_i / 1 \leq i \leq k \}$ the set of the k first words of the Ziv's factorization of α.

The words w_k, $k \in \mathbb{N}$, of the Ziv's factorization of α being all different , there exist an integer k_0 such that for all $k \geq k_0$, the following conditions (c4), (c5) et (c6) are satisfied

(c4) $\dfrac{(k+1)\log(n(k))}{n(k)} < \varepsilon'$

(c5) If we put $W'_k = \{ w \in W_k / |w| > l^2/\varepsilon' \}$, then

$$\sum_{w \in W'_k} |w| > (1-\varepsilon')n(k)$$

(c6) $f_C(a_1 a_2 \ldots a_{n(k)}) > 1 - \varepsilon'$ (this last condition follows from c2 and from the choice of the sequence α).

We fix the set C and the numbers ε, ε', l, k_0 for the sequel of this section.

Let us begin by a purely combinatorial lemma.

Lemma 1 Let j, l, p be three positive integers and C a set of words of length l. Let $L(j,p,C)$ the set of all the words $v \in A^*$ of length j which admit a factorization with the form

$$v = u_1 v_1 u_2 v_2 \ldots u_p v_p u_{p+1} \quad \text{whith} \quad v_i \in C, \ i = 1, 2, \ldots, p$$

Then $\text{card}(L(j,p,C)) \leq 2^{p+2(j-lp)}(\text{card}(C))^p$

<u>Proof</u> We have $|u_1u_2\ldots u_pu_{p+1}| = j-lp$

The word $u_1u_2\ldots u_pu_{p+1}$ having been choosed, there are C^p_{j-lp+p} ways to choose the places in this word to insert the words $v_1, v_2, \ldots, v_p$ and therefore

$$card(L(j,p,C)) \leq 2^{j-lp}C^p_{j-lp+p} (card(C))^p \leq 2^{p+2(j-lp)}(card(C))^p.$$

<u>Proposition 2</u>

For all $k \geq k_0$, let $W''_k = \{ w \in W'_k \ / \ f_C(w) > 1- \sqrt{\varepsilon'} \}$. Then

$$\sum_{w \in W''_k} |w| > (1 - 2 \sqrt{\varepsilon'})n(k)$$

<u>Proof</u> Let $k \geq k_0$ and let us note $n = n(k)$.

For all $i \in \{1,2,\ldots n-l+1\}$, let

$$\chi_i = \begin{cases} 1 \text{ if } a_ia_{i+1}\ldots a_{i+l-1} \in C \\ 0 \text{ else} \end{cases}$$

By the condition (c6) we have

$$\sum_{i=1}^{n-l+1} \chi_i > (1-\varepsilon')n$$

Hence there exist at most $\varepsilon'n$ indices $i \in \{1,2,\ldots,n-l+1\}$ such that $\chi_i = 0$.

Suppose that $v = a_ia_{i+1}\ldots a_{i+p} \in W'_k \setminus W''_k$. We have $f_C(v) \leq \sqrt{\varepsilon'}$ and consequently

for at least $\sqrt{\varepsilon'}|v|$ indices $j \in \{ i,\ldots, i+p-1 \}$ we have $\chi_j = 0$; hence

$$\sum_{v \in W'_k \setminus W''_k} \sqrt{\varepsilon'}|v| \leq \varepsilon'n$$

Making use of the condition (c5), we get

$$\sum_{v \in W_k \setminus W''_k} |v| \leq \sum_{v \in W'_k \setminus W''_k} |v| + \varepsilon'n \leq 2\sqrt{\varepsilon'}n$$

and this implies the proposition.

Proposition 3 Let $k \geq k_0$; W_k'' being defined as in the proposition 2, for all $j \in \mathbb{N}$, we have

$$\text{card}(W_k'' \cap A^j) \leq 2^{j(h+6\sqrt{\varepsilon'})}$$

Proof 1) Let us show first that every word $v \in W_k''$ has a factorization $v = sv_1v_2\cdots v_m t$ satisfying the conditions

i) $|s|, |t| < 1$

ii) $|v_i| = 1$, $i = 1, 2, \ldots, m$

iii) $\text{card}(\{\ i \in \{1, 2, \ldots, m\}\ /\ v_i \in C\ \}\ ) \geq (1-\sqrt{\varepsilon'})m$

Let $v = a_{i+1}a_{i+2}\cdots a_{i+p} \in W_k''$. By the definition of W_k'',

$$\sum_{j=1}^{p-1+1} \chi_{i+j} > (1-\sqrt{\varepsilon'})p \qquad (1)$$

There exist l different factorizations of v with the form $v = sv_1v_2\cdots v_m t$ with $|s|, |t| < 1$, $|v_i| = 1$, $i = 1, \ldots, m$. For each of these factorizations

$$m = \frac{p-|s|-|t|}{1} > \frac{p-2l}{1}$$

If the condition iii) was not satisfied by any of these l factorizations, the number of indices $j \in \{1, 2, \ldots, p-1+1\}$ such that $\chi_{i+j} = 0$ would be greater than $l\sqrt{\varepsilon'}\frac{p-2l}{1}$ and then we would get

$$\sum_{j=1}^{p-1+1} \chi_{i+j} < p-1+1-\sqrt{\varepsilon'}(p-2l) < p(1-\sqrt{\varepsilon'})$$

but this is impossible by the condition (1).

2) Let $v \in W_k'' \cap A^j$ and let $v = sv_1v_2 \ldots v_m t$ be a factorization of v with the properties i),ii),iii). Since $|v| = j$, we get the inequality $m > \frac{j-21}{1}$. Considering only words v_i belonging to C (and renumbering them if necessary), we get that there exists an integer p such that every word $v \in W_k'' \cap A^j$ has a factorization $v = u_1v_1u_2v_2 \ldots u_pv_pu_{p+1}$ satisfying the conditions

$$v_i \in C, \ i = 1,2,\ldots,p \ , \ \text{and} \ p > (1-\sqrt{\varepsilon'})(\frac{j-21}{1}) \qquad (2)$$

Since $v \in W_k''$, it follows from the condition (c5) that $j > 1^2/\varepsilon'$ and hence (making use of (2))

$$p > (1-\sqrt{\varepsilon'})(j/1)(1-21^2/j) > (1-2\sqrt{\varepsilon'})(j/1)$$

and therefore

$$j - 1p < 2\sqrt{\varepsilon'} j$$

Applying the lemma 1 and the condition (c3) we get

$$\text{card}(W_k'' \cap A^j) \leq 2^{p+4\sqrt{\varepsilon'} j} \cdot 2^{pl(h+\varepsilon')} \leq 2^{j(h+\varepsilon'+p/j+4\sqrt{\varepsilon'})} \qquad (3)$$

But by the condition (c1) we have

$$p/j \leq 1/l < \varepsilon' \qquad (4)$$

The proposition follows from (3) and (4).

<u>Proposition 4</u> For all $k \geq k_0$, $\frac{k\log k}{n(k)} < h+\varepsilon$.

<u>Proof</u>

1) Let $k \geq k_0$.

Let $k_1 = \text{card} (W_k \backslash W_k'')$ and $k_2 = \text{card}(W_k'')$. The mapping $x \to x\log x$ is convex and therefore

$$(k_1+k_2)\log(\frac{1}{2}(k_1+k_2)) \leq k_1\log k_1+k_2\log k_2$$

and then

$$k\log k \leq k_1\log k_1+k_2\log k_2+k \qquad (1)$$

2) For every $i = 1, 2, \ldots, n(k)$, let

$$b_i = \text{card}[(W_k \backslash W''_k) \cap A^i]$$

We have

$$\sum_{i=1}^{n(k)} b_i = k_1 \qquad (2)$$

and making use of the proposition 2

$$\sum_{i=1}^{n(k)} i b_i \leq 2\sqrt{\varepsilon}' n(k) \qquad (3)$$

The mapping $x \rightarrow x\log x$ being convex, we have

$$(\frac{1}{n(k)} \sum_{i=1}^{n(k)} b_i) \log(\frac{1}{n(k)} \sum_{i=1}^{n(k)} b_i) \leq \frac{1}{n(k)} \sum_{i=1}^{n(k)} b_i \log b_i \qquad (4)$$

But for all $i = 1, \ldots, n(k)$, $b_i \leq 2^i$ and then

$$\log b_i \leq i \qquad (5)$$

It follows from $(2), (3), (4), (5)$ que

$$k_1 \log k_1 \leq 2\sqrt{\varepsilon}' n(k) + k_1 \log(n(k)) \qquad (6)$$

3) For every $i = 1, 2, \ldots, n(k)$, let

$$c_i = \text{card}(W''_k \cap A^i)$$

We have the relations

$$\sum_{i=1}^{n(k)} c_i = k_2 \qquad (7)$$

$$\sum_{i=1}^{n(k)} i c_i \leq n(k) \qquad (8)$$

and, by proposition 3, for every $i = 1, \ldots, n(k)$,

$$\log(c_i) \leq i(h + 6\sqrt{\varepsilon}') \qquad (9)$$

From the relation (4) with c_i instead of b_i, it follows

$$k_2 \log k_2 \leq \sum_{i=1}^{n(k)} c_i \log c_i + k_2 \log(n(k)) \qquad (10)$$

hence, making use of the relations (8) et (9)

$$k_2 \log k_2 \leq (h + 6\sqrt{\varepsilon}') n(k) + k_2 \log(n(k)) \qquad (11)$$

Then, from the relations (1),(6) et (11) it follows

$$\frac{k\log k}{n(k)} \leq h+6\sqrt{\varepsilon}'+2\sqrt{\varepsilon}'+\frac{k\log n(k)+k}{n(k)}$$

and making use of the condition (c4) we get (supposing that we have chosen ε' small enough)

$$\frac{k\log k}{n(k)} \leq h+\varepsilon$$

<u>Corollary</u> For μ-almost-every sequence $\alpha = (a_n)_{n\in\mathbb{Z}}$

$$\lim\sup \frac{k\log k}{n(k,\alpha)} \leq h$$

<u>Proof</u> It is only necessary to remark that, by the proposition 1, μ-almost-every sequence α satisfies the condition (c0).

5. Majorizing the entropy.

The ideas of this section are essentially due to Gabriel[2].

We have defined previously the Ziv's factorization of an infinite sequence $\alpha = (a_n)_{n\in\mathbb{N}}$. Now let a word $u \in A^*$. We can define its Ziv's factorization $u = w_1 w_2 \cdots w_k w_{k+1}$ by defining w_i, $i = 1,\ldots,k$ as in the case of an infinite sequence, w_{k+1} being a prefix of one of the w_i, $i = 1,\ldots,k$. If w_{k+1} is the empty word , we shall say that the Ziv's factorization of u is *exact*. For all $u \in A^*$, let us note $k(u)$ the number of words in the Ziv's factorization of u.

<u>Lemma</u> <u>2</u> Let n be an integer. For every k, the number S_k of words $u \in A^n$ such that $k(u) \leq k$ is less or equal to $(2k)^k$.

<u>Proof</u> Let L_k be the set of all the words having an exact Ziv's factorization with exactly k factors. Then $card(L_1) = 2$ (since $card(A) = 2$). Moreover for all $k \geq 1$, we get the inequality

$$card(L_{k+1}) \leq 2k\,card(L_k)$$

Indeed, if $u = w_1 w_2 \cdots w_k w_{k+1} \in L_{k+1}$, then $u' = w_1 w_2 \cdots w_k \in L_k$ and the word w_{k+1} has the form $w_i a$ with $i \leq k$ and $a \in A$.

By induction, it follows that for all $k \in \mathbb{N}$, $\text{card}(L_k) \leq 2^k.(k-1)!$

But the number of the words **with a given length** n whose Ziv's factorization has k factors is less than the numbers of the words having an exact factorization with k factors (since it is always possible to extend an arbitrary word to obtain a word having an exact factorization with the same number of factors). Therefore

$$S_k \leq \sum_{i \leq k} 2^i (i-1)! < (2k)^k$$

Notation Let $(a_n)_{n \in \mathbb{Z}}$ be a doubly infinite sequence of elements of A. For any integer $n > 0$, let us note $u_n = a_1 a_2 \ldots a_n$.

Proposition 5 For μ-almost-every $(a_n)_{n \in \mathbb{Z}} \in A^{\mathbb{Z}}$

$$\liminf_n \frac{k(u_n)\log k(u_n)}{n} \geq h$$

Proof Let $\varepsilon > 0$ and let $\varepsilon' < \varepsilon$.

By the proposition 1, there exist $n_0 \in \mathbb{N}$ and a measurable set $B \subset A^{\mathbb{Z}}$ such that for all $n \geq n_0$ and all $(a_n)_{n \in \mathbb{Z}} \in B$, we have

$$\mu(B) \geq 1-\varepsilon' \tag{1}$$

$$\mu(a_1 a_2 \ldots a_n) \leq \frac{1}{2^{n(h-\varepsilon')}} \tag{2}$$

For all n, let $\beta(n)$ be the biggest integer such that

$$\frac{\beta(n)\log\beta(n)}{n} \leq h-\varepsilon \tag{3}$$

Let $n_1 \geq n_0$ such that for $n \geq n_1$ one has $h/\log(\beta(n)) < \varepsilon-\varepsilon'$ and

$$\sum_{n \geq n_1} \frac{1}{2^{n(\varepsilon-\varepsilon'-(h/\log(\beta(n))))}} \leq \varepsilon' \tag{4}$$

Let us define

$$B_n = \{ u \in A^n / k(u) \le \beta(n) \}$$

By the lemma 2

$$card(B_n) \le (2\beta(n))^{\beta(n)} \le 2^{n(h-\varepsilon+(h/\log(\beta(n))))}$$

we deduce (identifying B_n and the union of the corresponding cylinders)

$$\mu(B_n \cap B) \le 2^{n(h-\varepsilon+(h/\log(\beta(n))))} \cdot \frac{1}{2^{n(h-\varepsilon')}} \le \frac{1}{2^{n(\varepsilon-\varepsilon'-(h/\log(\beta(n))))}}$$

and making use of (4) it follows that

$$\sum_{n \ge n_1} \mu(B_n \cap B) \le \varepsilon' \qquad (5)$$

Let $C_{n_1} = \underset{n \ge n_1}{\cup} B_n$. Making use of (1) and (5), we get

$$\mu(C_{n_1}) \le 2\varepsilon' \qquad (6)$$

But for all $(a_n)_{n \in \mathbb{Z}} \notin C_{n_1}$ and all $n \ge n_1$ we have

$$\frac{k(u_n)\log k(u_n)}{n} > h-\varepsilon \qquad (7)$$

The numbers ε and ε' being chosen arbitrarily small the proposition

follows.

6. Conclusion and final remarks

6.1 Proof of the theorem 1

It results from the proposition 5 that for μ-almost-every $\alpha = (a_n)$

$$\underset{k}{\lim\inf} \frac{k\log k}{n(k,\alpha)} \ge h$$

Using the corollary of proposition 4 we get the theorem.

6.2 Remarks

1) It is easy to see that the conclusion of the theorem 1 can be given

the equivalent form: for μ-almost-every sequence $\alpha = (a_n)$

$$\underset{n}{\lim} \frac{k(u_n)\log k(u_n)}{n} = h$$

2) There is some computational evidence that, at least in the independent case, the practical estimations of the entropy are "too big". It seems that a more quickly convergent estimation of the entropy would be $\dfrac{k(u_n)[\log k(u_n)-c]}{n}$ where c is a constant to be determined.

References

[1] P. Billingsley, Ergodic theory and information, Wiley and Sons, Inc., 1965.
[2] P. Gabriel, Lecture in "Séminaire de théorie ergodique", Université de Paris VI, (non published).
[3] W. Parry, Entropy and generators in ergodic theory, W.A.Benjamin, Inc., 1969.
[4] C. Shannon, A mathematical theory of communication, Bell.System Tech.J., 27, p.379-423, p.623-656, 1948.
[5] J. Ziv and A. Lempel, Compression of individual sequences via variable-rate coding, IEEE Transactions on information theory, vol IT-24, no.5, p.530-536, sept.1978.

APPLICATIONS OF PHONETIC DESCRIPTION

Eric Laporte[1]
Laboratoire d'automatique documentaire et linguistique
Université Paris 7, 2, place Jussieu, 75221 PARIS CEDEX 05

Natural language, and in particular speech, is bound to have a prominent part in man-machine communication. Its industrial use is a major objective to which considerable technical means are being devoted in public and private computer research laboratories.

In the present state of scientific and technical knowledge in the domain of vocal output, recorded speech and compressed speech are adapted to a number of applications, and industry makes use of both on a large scale. This is not so with synthetic speech. Speech recording and compressing are techniques which enable storage of a bounded number of pre-chosen messages, and emission of any one of them. When a system has to produce various and numerous messages, storage is no longer possible and synthetic speech proper becomes the only solution. Synthetic speech will thus be useful in such applications as vocal output terminals. Variety and flexibility as regards (i) intonation, (ii) syntactic patterns and (iii) word choice are admittedly three prerequisites for making that type of application marketable. However, those three points remain challenges to fundamental research.

As far as speech recognition is concerned, many systems now on the market recognize a command language composed of up to a hundred elements or so. Continuous speech recognition systems will have to take into account a much greater variety of words and syntactic patterns than those command languages. That will require, in particular, a thorough knowledge of phonetic variations of words, since, of course, the variability of speech is a crucial problem for that category of applications.

Future systems having vocal input-output in English or in other languages will thus use accurate and concrete data about the pronunciation of oral messages. This paper is a general introduction to the main problems encountered in collecting such data and in giving them an appropriate representation. We discuss solutions to those problems and we mention the major computer applications requiring that description and representation work.

---

[1] I thank Maxine Eskenazi, who corrected a part of the English text of this paper; of course, she is not responsible for what is said.

Variability of speech

One of the specific features of speech, as opposed to written texts, is its variability. A spoken message is a function of the value of two parameters: the information content, and data about the speaker, since the pronunciation of a message depends on the speaker.

Geographical and social variations come into play. In those variations, each variant is related to a particular area or social level. Some of those variations are systematically represented in the whole lexicon: they occur with all words. For example, in French, some people roll their R's whereas others do not, in relation with their geographical and social origin and position. Other variations are isolated or lexical, i.e. they are a feature of only a specific, limited set of words: for instance, *either* is generally pronounced with [i:] in the United States and with [ai] in England. Those facts have repercussions on the way phonetic data can be used in computer systems and on the audience of those systems. If a phonetic description is restricted to a given region and social environment, the resulting applications will be only for the use of people who speak in that manner, i.e. people with a particular accent. This is a seriously unfavourable condition for commercial exploitation. If, on the contrary, a description extends over all of the regions where a language is spoken and all the social groups, the resultant variability reaches such proportions that one can hardly guarantee a full control on the description, at least for English and French. A more realistic approach is to take the middle course by choosing a rather widespread accent and taking account of the regions and social groups where speech is not too distant from that basic reference. Our work is thus focused on standard French, which can be approximately defined as that spoken on the television and radio, and which is essentially spoken in the Northern half of France. That work ought to be complemented by similar descriptions dedicated to regions where French is spoken in a markedly different way, notably the Southern half of France, Quebec, etc.

Besides geographical and social variations, there are individual phonetic variations: people differ in their way of pronouncing. Each person has his own voice. We all have specific phonetic habits, i.e. ways of pronouncing consonants or vowels. Some words undergo individual variations: in French, there are several common pronunciations for words like *mezzanine, vaciller* or *désuétude*. However, a given speaker is generally consistent in his manner of pronouncing each of them.

Finally, the pronunciation of a given word by a given person may also vary over time, depending on the speed and degree of care of the speaker and on other factors. For example, in French, liaisons may depend on the level of expression. Take the following sentence[2]:

Ce projet met ([], [t]) en jeu un investissement ([], ?[t]) important

In that sentence, liaisons are made only in a slightly formal style.

---

[2] Phonetic transcriptions are enclosed in square brackets []. The star * marks unacceptable utterances. When several pronunciations in the same context are considered, they are separated by commas and enclosed in parentheses. A question mark denotes an uncertainty in acceptability.

That relative freedom, i.e. the fact that several pronunciations are possible, marks a difference between speech and written language. That contrast is related to the fact that the former is less normalized than the latter. Written text production is generally more controlled, whereas oral discourse allows more spontaneity. That dissymmetry is also reflected in institutional and legal differences: the Académie française deals with spelling, and there are decrees about spelling, whereas all that has no phonetic counterpart. However, most of us do have a normative tendency: we often think there is a normalized pronunciation and try to find it. That attitude is hardly compatible with the activity advocated here, namely carrying out a mere description of facts. Consequently, any normative intention has to be dismissed for automatic speech processing, or for natural language processing as a whole.

At any rate, setting up norms for pronunciation would be a vast enterprise. If we admit phonetic dictionaries as a starting point for it, we face the problem that different dictionaries contradict each other. For instance, the French word *quai* is pronounced [ke] in some of them, [kɛ] in others, and still others consider both pronunciations acceptable, which is in keeping with current usage. Current usage could be used as a criterion to normalize pronunciation. Unfortunately it does not always concord with dictionaries: for instance, most dictionaries ignore the pronunciation of the French noun *cordillère* as *cordilière,* though it is common.

Moreover, even if such norms could be set up, that result would be of little interest, since current usage could not be modelled on artificial, imposed norms. On the contrary, it seems realistic to observe the variability and to take it into account: though considerable, it has its limits and can be described systematically.

Phonetics and prosody

If we are to automatically produce or recognize a spoken message, we need to know how to characterize it. That is one of the objectives of systematic description of pronunciation. In what terms can speech be described ? It can be characterized by several types of information. First, it can be represented by a phonetic transcription, more accurate and more explicit than common spelling:

Ce retard est dû à un incident technique

[søʀøtaredyaɛ̃nɛ̃sidãteknik]

Due to the variability of speech, one and the same message can be phonetically transcribed in several slightly different ways. The following phonetic sequence differs from the one above in that four unstressed vowels are more open:

[sœʀœtarɛdyaɛ̃nɛ̃sidãtɛknik]

Many other phonetic sequences, quite as acceptable as those, would feature so many ways of pronouncing the same message.

A phonetic sequence is an important element in characterizing a spoken message, but it is not sufficient. In addition to phonetic information, a spoken message has a 'melody', or prosody, which is crucial to understanding for it enables, among other things, the location of the limits of syntactic groups. It is not represented in phonetic sequences: it makes up an additional set of data, named prosodic data. The prosody of a spoken message can be defined as the stress, rhythm and intonation phenomena that are the result of three combined measurable parameters: duration, intensity and pitch.

- Every syllable in a sentence has a specific duration - in general different from that of neighbouring syllables -, which gives a rhythm to speech. For example, in French, the last syllable of certain words in a sentence has a generally longer duration than the average. In addition, speech is interspersed with pauses, which are characterized by their duration too.

- The sound volume of a spoken message undergoes rapid time variations between low values and louder values.

- The pitch of speech goes through similar variations which are easy to hear and can be measured after a spectral analysis of speech.

Since the prosodic features of a spoken message play a significant part in the understanding, they must be taken into account both in order to produce synthetic messages and to recognize messages uttered by people. For example, when an oral message is synthesized, if each of the prosodic parameters is given a constant value over time, the resulting speech is rhythmless, monotonous and difficult to understand.

The prosodic parameters of speech are represented neither in spelling, nor in phonetic transcriptions. The speech-synthesis systems which include a prosodic treatment generally use the following form of representation: prosodic markers are inserted at a number of spots in the phonetic transcription and enable the computation of the values of the prosodic parameters at every instant of the message. A phonetic transcription with prosodic markers is a rather complete representation of the pronunciation of a message, or at least enough for it to be synthesized with an acceptable quality.

The speech signal, or the result of a spectral analysis of it, is a more concrete representation of the pronunciation of a message. Translating automatically each of those two representations into the other is among the tasks to be achieved in order to make a success of speech synthesis and recognition. Needless to say, that difficult task can be performed satisfactorily only if both representations are of a good quality, and in particular

- if not too much information is lost during spectral analysis,

- and if phonetic transcriptions are correct and accurate.

The required quality is all the more difficult to obtain as phonetic transcriptions must often be elaborated automatically, without any improvements or finishing by hand.

In the following, we leave aside prosodic information to focus on phonetic information.

Main computer applications

We will survey the major applications making use of phonetic data. We will clarify which kind of information is needed and what the performances of existing and potential systems are.

First of all, we may consider the field of speech synthesis. Different kinds of systems can produce vocal output. Most of them include only a limited set of pre-recorded spoken messages and meet the requirements for commercially significant applications. Systems with more elaborate vocal output will be useful too: various, numerous messages consisting of sentences or texts can convey a more accurate and complex information. For example, the input of a text-to-speech system is unrestricted texts with their common spelling; the system utters those texts. Due to the variety of input texts, the corresponding phonetic texts and the values of the prosodic parameters must be obtained automatically from them. Some of those essential data are particularly difficult to compute (J. Allen, M.Sh. Hunnicutt and D. Klatt, 1987), namely: prosody, the pronunciation of some ambiguous words[3], and liaisons in the case of French. When text-to-speech systems work reliably, they will be very useful, e.g. to the blind.

The main problem with text-to-speech systems is the deep and manifold ambiguity of their input. That problem is not encountered in a second application: automatic generation of oral messages from concepts. The input of a concept-to-speech system (L. Danlos, F. Emerard and E. Laporte, 1986) consists of unambiguous, abstract representations of the information to be communicated to the user. Such a system produces and utters texts conveying that information. Since the input is unambiguous and the text of the messages is automatically generated by the system itself, all the syntactic information about it is directly available. Those syntactic data are used to give a prosody to the text, to determine the liaisons and to obtain the pronunciations of words like *lead,* which are spelt the same and pronounced differently. Those systems are necessarily domain-restricted and may be built only after a detailed syntactic and semantic study of their domain. They are not found on the market yet.

A text-to-speech system as well as a generator of oral messages requires a phonetic dictionary in order to determine the pronunciation of the words. Another solution would be to use a set of rules which computes the pronunciation into a phonetic code, i.e. a phonetizer. In languages like Italian and Spanish, that solution can work. In languages like French and English, the mapping between spelling and phonetic transcriptions is so irregular that even the rule-based solution, to work reliably, would imply the use of a dictionary: that dictionary would provide the phonetic data in a computerized form, make easier the consultation of the data and help to establish lists of

---

[3] For example, in English, the two words written *lead* are pronounced *leed* and *led*: they are homographic, non-homophonic words.

exceptions. Furthermore, in those languages, a reliable phonetizer is more difficult to maintain than a reliable dictionary (see below).

Another problem to be solved is that of vocal input. The vocal input recognized by existing systems is usually restricted to a set of vocal commands used to control some device. Those systems meet an increasing commercial demand and are more and more industrialized. Voice-activated typewriters will have to recognize a much more complex input: in that foreseen application, the system trancribes into written language texts uttered by the user. That input can only be minimally restricted, as it is the case for any system analyzing human input. Therefore, a realistic voice-activated typewriter should take into account the variability of speech and be able to process a wide range of data. When a message can be pronounced in several ways, all those forms should be recognizable: the message would probably have a single internal representation, and the system should be able to match it with the forms encountered. In addition to a phonetic dictionary, an account of variations is thus required (P.S. Cohen and R.L. Mercer, 1974; J.E. Shoup, 1980). Besides purely phonetic variations, speech undergoes slight acoustic variations. Those problems and others explain why speech recognition is only at its beginning.

Among the applications of phonetic description, computer-aided spelling correction is the most feasible in the near future. Generally speaking, that task can be performed in many ways. However, the framework is roughly as follows:

- detect the words that are most likely to be incorrect,

- select a set of possible correct forms,

- choose the correct form among that set.

Only the second step can be done with a phonetic method (E. Laporte and M. Silberztein, 1988). That method is based on the following fact: in French and in English, a significant proportion of spelling errors leave the pronunciation unchanged or change it very little. For example, if the French word *système* is misspelt as *systhème,* the resulting string can still be read aloud and pronounced in the same way as the original word. Similarly, spelling the word *illimité* as *ilimmité* hardly affects the pronunciation of that word. Those errors, once discovered, can be corrected by computing the pronunciation of the incorrect word and finding its spelling(s). An unknown-word phonetizer is required, because a phonetic dictionary does not tell the pronunciation of misspelt words. We implemented that method and obtained satisfactory results. When the spelling of a word is not completely clear, which often happens, the phonetizer provides several solutions. We also needed a reversed phonetic dictionary in order to find out the correct spellings for a given pronunciation. That reversed phonetic dictionary was automatically built from the dictionary DELAP[4].

---

[4] Dictionnaire Electronique du LADL pour la Phonémique (the LADL's electronic dictionary for phonemics).

Problems of maintenance

Any natural-language computer system needs maintenance as long as it is used. With the evolution of terminology and users' needs, new words appear and it must be possible to update the linguistic data of a system in proportion. Moreover, errors need be corrected as soon as discovered. For example, if the linguistic data take the form of a dictionary, each new word must be entered with relevant information. That information must be coded so as to be machine-usable. The efficient working of the system depends on the quality and consistency of that coding. In particular, the coding should rest on definite methods and not on tricks of little generality. This is why a thorough analysis of linguistic facts is necessary to develop methods of coding. While the system is used, unusual cases inevitably show up: a method of coding improvised with no such preliminary analysis cannot be general enough to handle adequately all of them.

Maintenance is also easier if the descriptions of words are independent from one another. This is the case with a phonetic dictionary. Whenever a word is added, modified, corrected or deleted, no side effects arise: the coding of other words need not be reconsidered. Due to that property, dictionaries are comparatively easy to maintain and update. Rule-based algorithms do not offer the same advantage. Take the case of a rule-based phonetizer, i.e. an algorithm and a set of rules and exceptions designed to compute phonetic transcriptions of words from their spelling. A lot of rule-based phonetizers for French have been written since D. Teil (1969). A phonetizer for French words may state the following rules and exceptions:

Rule R_1.

The letter *s* is transcribed [s].

Example: *piste* [pist].

Exception E_1 to rule R_1.

If *s* occurs between two vowels, it is transcribed [z].

Example: *rasoir* [razwar].

Exception E_2 to exception E_1.

If *s* occurs after one of a number of prefixes like *para-*, it is transcribed [s].

Example: *parasol* [parasɔl].

Exception E_3 to exception E_2.

If the word figures in a list of few words like *parasite* and its derivations, it is transcribed [z].

Example: *parasite* [parazit].

In a set of rules and exceptions, the smallest modifiable elements are not lexical items, but rules and exceptions. A given rule or exception generally concerns a lot of lexical items. Moreover, rules and exceptions are hierarchically organized: rules have exceptions; as the example above shows, the exceptions can have exceptions in their turn, and so on. In such a system, whenever a rule or exception is modified, added, corrected or deleted, that can alter the processing of several words: (i) those concerned by the rule and (ii) those concerned by hierarchically related rules or exceptions. Unfortunately, if no dictionary is available, nothing provides the list of words concerned by a given rule. Therefore, for all practical purposes, there are no methods of evaluating the consequences of a modification in a set of rules, and a modification can entail unexpected side effects. For instance, exception E_2 above should list the prefixes that can be followed by an [s]-sounding intervocalic letter *s*:

para-	*parasol*
aéro-	*aérosol*
ortho-	*orthosympathique*
a-	*asymétrique*
déca-	*décasyllabe*
etc.	

Making out that list is a complex operation, and so is any modification made to it. For instance, assume that the prefix *dé-* is inserted in that list, on account of the verb *désolidariser* which is pronouced with [s]. Then exception E_3 must be reconsidered: words like *désembuer* are pronounced with [z] and must be listed on E_3, otherwise a systematic error slips into the system. In the last analysis, such difficulties come from the fact that the data are organized in rules and exceptions. In contrast, the data organization in a phonetic electronic dictionary reflects the fact that the pronunciation of *désolidariser* and that of *désembuer* are independent pieces of information and should be considered separately, at least for the purpose of maintenance.

A rule-based phonetizer and a phonetic dictionary are equally powerful formal devices. Both return phonetic transcriptions of their input; there may be errors in both. The differences lie on other points. A dictionary is generally better adapted to maintenance and updating. A rule-based algorithm usually has a higher time and space efficiency.

Free phonetic variations

There are many examples of phonetic variations. We mentioned geographical and social ones, individual ones, and those related to speed or style. When no accurate data about variations are available, one cannot but ignore them. This amounts to arbitrarily choosing one of the variants and discarding the others whenever such a variation is met. However, variations can be systematically described and given formal representations in electronic dictionaries.

Few phonetic variations are absolutely free variations: the variants are usually not perfectly interchangeable. They may be related to distinct areas, social groups, speakers, styles, levels of expression... Those factors could hardly be taken into account both systematically and in detail. That would involve relating each variant to a number of factors. But if the variants are considered free, they can be systematically described. That amounts to neglecting the slight differences in the use of the variants, but not their phonetic differences. The following remark justifies that approximation. The slight differences in the use of that type of variants hardly play a part in the process of understanding a spoken message: they may at most arouse various impressions or produce stylistic effects. In contrast, the phonetic differences between variants can be important. For example, in the French sentence *Guy va prendre du temps,* the suffix *-re* in *prendre* can be pronounced or not. The corresponding phonetic transcriptions are noticeably different:

[givaprădr∅dytă]

[givaprăndytă]

In particular, the latter variant has one syllable less than the former, which is of consequence for the purpose of automatic acoustic recognition. The variants present a slight difference in their use: the first sounds more formal and the other more ordinary. However, as things stands so far, such a distinction need not be taken into consideration and we consider the variants equivalent.

On that basis, we undertook to describe systematically the phonetic variations of French. The results are part of the dictionary DELAP.

In cases of limited variations, a list of the variants suffices. This is the case for words like *mezzanine* or *vaciller.* In the case where all intermediates between two variants are acceptable, we are facing a problem. Take for example the French word *aïkido.* In that word, the letter *i* can form a separate syllable or not, and it can also be pronounced in an intermediate way between those extreme possibilities, the number of syllables of the word being then unclear. Another example is the word *emprunt.* The vowel *un* can be pronounced as [ɛ̃], [œ̃] or as any intermediate. In the DELAP, words like *mezzanine, vaciller* or *aïkido* have two entries each.

When too many words present a given phonetic variation, it becomes more and more tedious, and eventually impracticable, to duplicate their lexical entries. The French verb *lier,* for instance, has either one or two syllables: the letter *i* can form the centre of a separate syllable or not. That particular variation affects a few dozens of words. Other types of variations may affect even several thousands of words: *illégal* is pronounced either with a simple or double consonant; *louer* is pronounced either with one or two syllables; *arrêt, série* and *illégal,* with a closed [e] or with an open [ɛ]; *colis,* with a closed [o] or with an open [ɔ]; *mener,* with a closed [∅], with an open [œ] or with the first *e* elided. For each of those words, all of the variants could be listed, but it is clearly simpler to use special symbols, for example a phoneme /e/ which stands for both closed [e] and open [ɛ]. That type of solution was first put forward and investigated by phonologists, and it now meets the needs of spoken natural language processing. In consequence, a symbolic system with a phonemic alphabet and transducers was designed and implemented. The symbols are named phonemes and stand for the phonetic segments making up phonetic transcriptions, but are more abstract. Phonemic transcriptions in the form of strings of phonemes are assigned to words: for instance, /seri/ to *série*. That solution thus makes use of an abstract level of representation which we name phonemic level. Phonemic transcriptions can be translated into phonetic transcriptions by transducers which are given a mathematical, automatable form. Then, a phonemic form /seri/ generates [seri] and [sɛri], which are two extreme pronunciations of the noun *série*. Such a system is clearly a better method of coding than multiple lexical entries, because it makes maintenance easier.

However, building a phonemic system implies many choices. Little is known about phonetic variations, and standard solutions are not in use yet. Given that fact, much uncertainty remains with regard to the phonemic alphabet. In other words, one does not know in what terms to encode the pronunciation of words.

Conditioned phonetic variations

The preceding section is dedicated to free variations, i.e. those for which variants are interchangeable or have only negligible differences of use. Speech recognition requires data about free variations, since the speaker can pronounce any variant, and all of them must be recognizable. In a speech-synthesis system, one of the variants can be arbitrarily chosen, since all are acceptable and equivalent. Data about free variations are therefore less useful for synthesis.

In contrast, conditioned variations must be known in detail both for speech recognition and for speech synthesis. An example is the conjugation of the French verb *manier*. In the conjugated forms, diverse suffixes are appended to a stem. That stem has two variants: in the first variant, the letter *i* forms the centre of a separate syllable, and in the other it does not. The variants are mutually exclusive and their use is conditioned by the suffix. If the suffix is void or begins with a consonant, the form with syllabic *i* is always used, and if it begins with a vowel, the form with non-syllabic *i* is always used:

Guy manie un levier	syllabic *i*
Guy maniait un levier	non-syllabic *i*

Both forms of the stem are phonetic variants of the same element, but are not interchangeable: their use depends on specific conditions. In that example, the conditions regard the suffix appended to the variable stem.

There are many examples of conditioned variations. Whether the letter *e*, occurring in words like *presque* and *remis*, should be elided or not, may be dependent upon the context. In both of those words, the underlined *e* can be pronounced or elided. However, in the following sentence: *Il est presque remis*, at most one of the two underlined *e* can be elided. Both variants of each word are therefore not used in exactly the same conditions. The following sentences are another example:

Guy vient d'arriver

Guy vient de partir

In the latter, the preposition *de* is usually pronounced [n], whereas that never occurs in the former. That difference is due to the phonetic context of *de* in those sentences and in others of the same type.

Most conditioned phonetic variations are systematic, i.e. they extend over a large part of the lexicon. Hence they take on particular importance. The variation of *manier* concerns about 250 verbs ending in *-ier*; those of mute *e* in *presque remis* and of *de* in *Guy vient de partir* are very general too. Because of that general distribution, they can be profitably represented with phonemes and transducers, in a similar way as free variations in the last section. For instance, the phonetic segment [n] in *Guy vient de partir* can be symbolized by the phoneme /d/; a transducer can produce the relevant phonetic sequence [givjɛ̃npartir] from the phonemic sequence.

However, a conditioned phonetic variation is more complex than a free one. A full description of a conditioned variation specifies not only the phonetic form of all variants but also their conditions of use. That receives a natural framework in a phonemic system: the conditions of use of the variants are easily expressed in the transducer that translates phonemic sequences into phonetic sequences. Thus, the theory of formal languages provides appropriate tools for representing phonetic variations. The main problem is that a significant amount of descriptive work will be necessary to know the variations accurately and systematically.

Conditioned phonetic variations: some awkward examples

In the above examples, the conditions of use of variants are related to their phonetic context. Other variations are conditioned by further linguistic elements, such as grammatical and syntactic information. The liaison in French is an example. In a given sentence, whether a liaison is always made, sometimes made or never made depends on several criteria. (i) The initial phoneme of the following word is of course one of those criteria:

C'est son ([], *[n]) *jouet favori*

C'est son (*[], [n]) *amusement favori*

In the first sentence, the liaison is never made; in the other, it is always made. (ii) The syntactic relations between the two adjacent words are the deciding factor in the following pairs of sentences:

C'est son (*[], [n]) *amusement favori*

Il a fait un son ([], *[n]) *amusant*

Guy a un (*[], [n]) *aussi grand projet qu'Anne*

Luc en a un ([], *[n]) *aussi*

(iii) The third factor is the least easy to see. Here, it is the inflectional features of the first word that are decisive:

Luc a un travers ([], *[z]) *insupportable*

Luc a des travers ([], [z]) *insupportables*

Il y avait là un corps ([], ?*[z]) *inerte*

Il y avait là des corps ([], [z]) *inertes*

In a frozen expression, the possible liaisons depend on the expression and on its syntactic type:

Il n'a qu'un mot ([], *[t]) *à dire*

Il traduit mot (*[], [t]) *à mot*

The three pronunciations of the French numeral *six* offer another well-known example. They appear respectively in the following three sentences:

Luc a six billes à la main	[si] *[siz] *[sis]
Luc a six ans	*[si] [siz] *[sis]
Luc en a six à la main	*[si] *[siz] [sis]

The use of [sis] is conditioned by the syntax of the sentence. The numeral *quatre-vingts* is composed of 3 syllables, whereas the phrase *quatre vins* may be pronounced 2-syllabic. That difference is connected to an essentially syntactic fact: *quatre-vingts* is a fixed phrase and *quatre vins* is not. There is a similar difference between *demi-heure*, where *i* can be either syllabic or non-syllabic, and *demi-abricot*, where *i* is always syllabic.

In all those examples, the pronunciation of words or phrases depends on various kinds of linguistic information, some of which are rather abstract. That linguistic information is not explicitly represented in written or spoken texts. This is why that kind of phenomena is so awkward for natural language processing. A system can take such facts into account only if the following constraint is satisfied: whenever the pronunciation depends on some other linguistic information, that information must be available at the moment of processing the phonetic data. This is a strong restriction on architecture of programs.

Conclusion

Computer applications with vocal input-output in natural languages will involve the use of accurate phonetic data, and in particular of data about phonetic variations. Those variations can be described, analyzed and given a formal representation with simple tools from computer theory: strings of symbols and transductions. However, gathering those basic phonetic data also implies a systematic study of the lexicon of the languages. At that expense, some of the specific difficulties of speech, as opposed to written texts, can be overcome.

References

J. ALLEN, M.Sh. HUNNICUTT and D. KLATT, 1987, *From text to speech. The MITalk system,* Cambridge : Cambridge University Press.

P.S. COHEN and R.L. MERCER, 1974, "The Phonological Component of an Automatic Speech-Recognition System", *Proceedings of IEEE Symposium on Speech Recognition,* pp. 177-188.

L. DANLOS, F. EMERARD and E. LAPORTE, 1986, "Generation of Spoken Messages from Semantic Representations : A Semantic-Representation-to-Speech System", *Proceedings of COLING 1986,* Bonn.

E. LAPORTE and M. SILBERZTEIN, 1988, "Correction orthographique lexicale par phonétisation", *Actes de la Convention "Intelligence artificielle",* Paris.

J.E. SHOUP, 1980, "Phonological Aspects of Speech Recognition", in Wayne A. LEA (ed.), *Trend in Speech Recognition,* Prentice-Hall, pp. 125-138.

D. TEIL, 1969, *Etude de génération synthétique de parole à l'aide d'un ordinateur,* Thèse Conservatoire national des arts et métiers, Paris.

Sequence Comparison: Some Theory and Some Practice

Imre Simon[*]
Instituto de Matemática e Estatística
Universidade de São Paulo
05508 São Paulo, SP, Brasil

Abstract

A brief survey of the theory and practice of sequence comparison is made focusing on diff, the UNIX[1] file difference utility.

1 Sequence comparison

Sequence comparison is a deep and fascinating subject in Computer Science, both theoretical and practical. However, in our opinion, neither the theoretical nor the practical aspects of the problem are well understood and we feel that their mastery is a true challenge for Computer Science.

The central problem can be stated very easily: find an algorithm, as efficient and practical as possible, to compute a longest common subsequence (lcs for short) of two given sequences[2].

As usual, a subsequence of a sequence is another sequence obtained from it by deleting some (not necessarily contiguous) terms. Thus, both en␣pri and en␣pai are longest common subsequences of sequence␣comparison and theory␣and␣practice.

---

[*]Part of this work was done while the author was visiting the Université de Rouen, in 1987. That visit was partially supported by FAPESP.

[1]UNIX is a trademark of Bell Laboratories

[2]The sequences we consider are usually called words. We avoid this terminology since it might lead to confusion because of the widespread misuse of the term subword (meaning a segment or a factor instead of a subsequence).

It turns out that this problem has many, many applications in many, many apparently unrelated fields, such as computer science, mathematics, molecular biology, speech recognition, gas chromatography, bird song analysis, etc. A comprehensive study of the role of the problem in these fields and how it is coped with in each of them can be found in the beautiful book of Sankoff and Kruskal [37].

In particular, in computer science the problem has at least two applications. The main one is a file comparison utility, nowadays universally called diff, after its popularization through the UNIX operating system. This tool is intensively used to discover differences between versions of a text file. In this role it is useful in keeping track of the evolution of a document or of a computer program. It is also used as a file compression utility, since many versions of a (long) file can be represented by storing one (long) version of it and many (short) scripts of transforming the stored version in the remaining ones. Another aplication in computer science is to approximate string matching used, for instance, in the detection of misspelled versions of names. It should be noted, however, that sequence comparison is not the main tool to solve this very important problem. For more details the reader is referred to [16].

An interesting aspect of the problem is that it can be solved by a simple and perhaps even intuitive 'folklore' algorithm based on a dynamic programming approach. This appealing algorithm has been discovered many, many times. Indeed, it has been discovered by engineers, by biologists and by computer scientists, in Russia, Japan, United States, France and Canada in the period 1968 to 1975. The first publication of the algorithm seems to be, according [37], in a 1968 paper by the russian engineer Vintsyuk [45].

The big challenge to computer science comes from the complexity of the folklore algorithm. Indeed, it requires time proportional to the product of the lengths of the sequences, and no essentially better practical algorithm is known. The question is to search for a possible algorithm which is simultaneously efficient and practical.

As far as we know, the existence of a linear algorithm has not been ruled out. Neither has been found a practical algorithm which worst case time complexity is better than $O(mn)$, where m and n are the lengths of the given sequences. There exists, however, an algorithm of time complexity $O(n^2/\log n)$ for pairs of sequences of length n over a fixed finite alphabet, discovered by Masek and Paterson [29]. This algorithm is not suitable for practical purposes but its existence is a hint that better algorithms than the ones in current use must exist.

All told, a very good start would be to find out whether or not there exists a linear time algorithm to compute a longest common subsequence of two given sequences over two letters. We get a more modest but still very interesting start by replacing "linear time" for "time complexity $O(n \log n)$". Here, the time bounds should be measured on a random access machine under the unit-cost model.

A weaker version, already answered by Masek and Paterson, has been proposed by D. E. Knuth in a technical report coauthored with V. Chvátal and D. A. Klarner in 1972 [9]:

Problem 35.   Greatest common substrings.
   It is possible to find the longest common subsequence of two sequences of a's and b's in a time proportional to the product of their lengths. Can one do better?
Note: aba is a subsequence of aabbbba.

Incidentally, this seems to be the first reference to the problem and to the folklore algorithm within Computer Science.

2   Some theory

We begin this section with the presentation of the folklore algorithm which is the starting point for most of the known algorithms to find an lcs of two given sequences.

Let $u = u_1 u_2 \cdots u_n$ and $v = v_1 v_2 \cdots v_m$ be sequences of lengths n and m over an alphabet A. We assume that each u_i and v_j is a letter in A. The folklore algorithm consists of computing the length $d(i,j)$ of an lcs of $u_1 \cdots u_i$ and $v_1 \cdots v_j$. This can be done by observing that $d(0,0) = 0$ and by repeatedly applying the formula:

$$d(i,j) = \begin{cases} 1 + d(i-1, j-1) & \text{if } u_i = v_j, \\ \max\{ d(i-1, j), d(i, j-1) \} & \text{if } u_i \neq v_j. \end{cases}$$

Having computed the matrix d the length of an lcs of u and v is $d(n,m)$ and a common subsequence of length $d(n,m)$ can be computed easily proceeding backwards: from $d(n,m)$ to $d(0,0)$. Figure 1 shows an application of the folklore algorithm.

The time complexity of this algorithm is clearly $O(nm)$; actually this time does not depend on the sequences u and v themselves but only on

	s	e	q	u	e	n	c	e	⊔	c	o	m	p	a	r	i	s	o	n
t	0	0	0	0	0	0	0	0	0	0	0	0	0	0	0	0	0	0	0
h	0	0	0	0	0	0	0	0	0	0	0	0	0	0	0	0	0	0	0
e	0	1	1	1	1	1	1	1	1	1	1	1	1	1	1	1	1	1	1
o	0	1	1	1	1	1	1	1	1	1	2	2	2	2	2	2	2	2	2
r	0	1	1	1	1	1	1	1	1	1	2	2	2	2	3	3	3	3	3
y	0	1	1	1	1	1	1	1	1	1	2	2	2	2	3	3	3	3	3
⊔	0	1	1	1	1	1	1	1	2	2	2	2	2	2	3	3	3	3	3
a	0	1	1	1	1	1	1	1	2	2	2	2	2	3	3	3	3	3	3
n	0	1	1	1	1	2	2	2	2	2	2	2	2	3	3	3	3	3	4
d	0	1	1	1	1	2	2	2	2	2	2	2	2	3	3	3	3	3	4
⊔	0	1	1	1	1	2	2	2	3	3	3	3	3	3	3	3	3	3	4
p	0	1	1	1	1	2	2	2	3	3	3	3	4	4	4	4	4	4	4
r	0	1	1	1	1	2	2	2	3	3	3	3	4	4	5	5	5	5	5
a	0	1	1	1	1	2	2	2	3	3	3	3	4	5	5	5	5	5	5
c	0	1	1	1	1	2	3	3	3	4	4	4	4	5	5	5	5	5	5
t	0	1	1	1	1	2	3	3	3	4	4	4	4	5	5	5	5	5	5
i	0	1	1	1	1	2	3	3	3	4	4	4	4	5	5	6	6	6	6
c	0	1	1	1	1	2	3	3	3	4	4	4	4	5	5	6	6	6	6
e	0	1	1	1	2	2	3	4	4	4	4	4	4	5	5	6	6	6	6

Figure 1: An example for the folklore algorithm

their lengths. By choosing carefully the order of computing the $d(i,j)$'s one can execute the above algorithm in space $O(n + m)$. Even an lcs can be obtained within this time and space complexities but this requires a clever subdivision of the problem [21].

An important property of this dynamic programming algorithm is that it can easily be generalized to computing the minimum cost of editing u into v given (possibly different) costs of the operations: changing a letter into another and deleting or inserting a letter [46].

The literature contains a large number of variants of this algorithm, most of them are recorded in the bibliography. Just to give some idea about the various time bounds Table 1 lists a few results, where we assume that u and v have the same length n. In the table p denotes the length of the result (an lcs of u and v). Also, r denotes the number of matches, i.e. the number of pairs $(i,j) \in [1,n] \times [1,n]$ for which $u_i = v_j$.

Hunt and Szymanski(77) [25]	$O((r + n) \log n)$
Hirschberg(77) [19]	$O(pn + n \log n)$
Hirschberg(77) [19]	$O(((n + 1 - p)p \log n)$
Nakatsu et al.(82) [33]	$O(n(n - p))$
Hebrard(84) [17]	$O(pn)$

Table 1: Time complexities of some lcs algorithms

None of the algorithms in Table 1 have worst case time complexity better than $O(n^2)$, some are even worse. This can be seen by observing that the value of p varies between 0 and n, while that of r varies between 0 and n^2 and their average value, for pairs of sequences over a fixed alphabet, is proportional, respectively, to n and n^2. It is important to note, however, that, for particular cases, some of the algorithms might use considerably less time than in the worst case. A lively description, from a unified viewpoint, of two of the main algorithms and some variations can be found in [7], a recent paper by Apostolico and Guerra.

The most interesting theoretical result is that of Masek and Paterson [29]. Carefully using subdivision techniques similar to the ones used in the "Four russian's algorithm" they transformed the folklore algorithm into one with time complexity $O(n^2/\log n)$. This is indeed the only evidence that there exist faster algorithms than the folklore one.

Before talking about lower bounds we would like to clarify the model we think is appropriate for the lcs problem. First, the time complexity should be measured on a random access machine under the unit cost model. This seems to be the correct model because we are interested in practical algorithms and this is the closest we can get to existing computers. Second, the time complexity should be measured in terms of the total size, say t, of the input, instead of simply considering the length, say n, of the input sequences. This is a delicate point. For sequences over a known and fixed alphabet we can consider $t = n$ and this was the case considered until now. The other common assumption is to consider sequences over a potentially unbounded alphabet. In this case we assume that the letters are coded over some known, fixed and finite auxiliary alphabet; hence, to represent n different symbols we need size $t \in \Omega(n \log n)$. Thus, measuring complexity in terms of n or t turn out to be very different!

This model adjusts very well to the current philosophy of text files whenever each line is considered as a letter. In particular, this is the case of the file comparison utilities, our main example for the unbounded alphabet model. In essence we propose that in this case complexity should be measured in terms of the length of the files instead of their number of lines. The main consequence of this proposal is that it increases considerably, but within reasonable bounds, the world of linear algorithms: just for one example, sorting the lines of a text file can be done in linear time [3,30].

The existing lower bounds for the complexity of the longest common subsequence problem [14,1,47,20] are based on restricted models of computations and do not apply to the model we just proposed. This point seems to be responsible for a certain amount of confusion because sometimes the known lower bounds tend to be interpreted outside the model for which they were obtained. Indeed, as far as we are aware of, no known lower bound excludes the existence of a linear algorithm in the sense just outlined.

Another very interesting, apparently difficult and little developed area is the probabilistic analysis of the quantities envolved in the lcs problem. Let $f(n,k)$ be the average length of the lcs of two sequences of length n over an alphabet A of k letters (the uniform distribution on A^n is assumed). The function $f(n,k)$ has been explicitly computed for small values of n and k in [11]. On the asymptotic side it is known that for every k there exists a constant c_k such that

$$\lim_{n \to \infty} \frac{f(n,k)}{n} = \sup_n \frac{f(n,k)}{n} = c_k.$$

Thus, fixing the finite alphabet A, the length of an lcs of two random sequences in A^n is ultimately proportional to n.

The exact determination of c_k seems elusive and only lower and upper bounds are known for small values of k. Some results in this direction appear in Table 2. For more details, see [37,13,10].

An interesting conjecture was made by Sankoff and Mainville [37]:

$$\lim_{k \to \infty} \sqrt{k} c_k = 2.$$

We close this section mentioning five results related, in one way or another, to the lcs problem.

A very important subproblem is obtained by restricting the input to permutations (sequences in which each letter occurs at most once). This case was solved by Szymansky [42] in time $O(n \log n)$. Such an algorithm is also contained in work of Hunt and Szymanski [25] and that of Hunt and

85

k	lower bound	upper bound
2	0.76	0.86
5	0.51	0.67
10	0.40	0.54
15	0.32	0.46

Table 2: Some upper and lower bounds for c_k

McIlroy [24]. It is an open problem whether or not the case of permutations can be done in linear time on the model we proposed.

A further restriction leads to yet another very important subproblem. This is obtained if we consider $(1, 2, \ldots, n)$ as one of the permutations, assuming, of course, the alphabet $[1, n]$. Then an lcs is just a longest increasing subsequence of the second permutation and this problem is part of a very rich theory of representations of the symmetric group using Young tableaux extensively studied by A. Young, G de B. Robinson, C. E. Schensted and M. P. Schützenberger. A survey focusing on the computational aspects can be found in Knuth's book [26] from which Fredman [14] extracted an algorithm to solve the longest increasing subsequence problem. His algorithm runs in time $O(n \log n)$ and he also derives $n \log n$ as a lower bound for the problem. But, beware, the lower bound does not apply to our model! Using the theory of Young tablaux one can compute the number of permutations of $[1, n]$ which has a longest increasing subsequence of any given length. Extensive calculations can be found in [8]. However, the expected value of the length of a longest increasing subsequence of a permutation of length n is not known but the data compiled in [8] indicate that this value is approximately $2\sqrt{n}$.

The third related problem is obtained if we look for a longest common segment of two sequences instead of a longest common subsequence. In [12] a linear algorithm was obtained to solve this problem.

The fourth related problem is obtained by considering mini-max duality: instead of looking for the longest common subsequence what about a shortest uncommon subsequence? In 1984 the author solved this problem with an algorithm of time complexity $O(|A| + |u| + |v|)$. More precisely, this (unpublished) linear algorithm computes a shortest sequence which distinguishes the sequences u and v over the alphabet A, that is to say, a shortest sequence which is a subsequence of exactly one of the unequal sequences u and v. For instance, consider sequence␣comparison and theory␣and␣practice: eee distinguishes them while cc does not. A shortest distinguisher is given by d.

The last related problem is a negative result (from our point of view). It was shown by Maier [28] that deciding whether or not a finite set of sequences has a common subsequence of length k is an NP-complete problem. Other related NP-complete problems can be found in [15].

3   Some practice

In this section we restrict ourselves to some practical aspects of file comparison utilities, focusing especially on the UNIX command diff.

A file comparison utility should determine the differences between two text files. But what is the difference of two text files? Indeed, our intuitive notion of such a difference is an elusive concept and it is difficult to define it. To cope with this it became common practice to consider entire lines as indivisible objects. Then it seems that the best results are obtained if one finds a longest common subsequence of lines and then anything not in this lcs is declared a difference.

The first (and still the best) file comparison utility was included in UNIX around 1976. Since then file comparison became a standard tool and with the proliferation of microcomputers many programs turned up. These are usually called diff, but most of them do not determine a true lcs; consequently they easily missynchronize. On the other hand, some of them are very fast and work well for many pairs of (real text) files. Many of these programs are based on [18].

One aspect of the file comparison programs for microcomputers is worth mentioning: their output is sometimes more suggestive (for a human) of the differences than the output of the original diff. Indeed, a good way of pinpoiting the differences seems to be a simultaneous listing of both files, indicating whether each line is common to both or exclusive to one of them. Long blocks of lines in the same class might be abbreviated by showing only their first and last lines. In contrast, the output of diff is thoroughly influenced by the intricacies of machine transformation of one file in another and this restricts, in our opinion, its potential as a tool for remembering or discovering the changes during the evolution of a file.

The algorithm actually used by diff is described by Hunt and McIlroy in [24]; its basic idea is attributed to unpublished work of H. S. Stone who generalized an $O(n \log n)$ solution of the most important particular case (the restriction of the problem to permutations) by T. G. Szymanski [42]. The resulting algorithm is very similar to the one in [25]; it is also described in [2].

The first practical concession of diff is that it hashes the lines of the files. This is handy because it reduces significantly the volume of information to deal with. On the other hand, the hashing might introduce false matches caused by collisions; these are detected during the last phase when the computed lcs is checked in the files themselves. If false matches occur the corresponding lines are considered as differences. Consequently, it might happen that the reported common subsequence of lines is not a longest one. These events seems to be very rare in practice and the advantages of hashing greatly outweight its shortcomings.

The key concept in the algorithm is that of a k-candidate. Returning to our notations in the previous section, a k-candidate is a pair of positions (i,j) such that $u_i = v_j$ and

$$k = d(i,j) = d(i,j-1) + 1 = d(i-1,j) + 1 = d(i-1,j-1) + 1.$$

It follows that every lcs of $u_1 \ldots u_i$ and $v_1 \ldots v_j$ is the concatenation of an lcs of $u_1 \ldots u_{i-1}$ and $v_1 \ldots v_{j-1}$ with the letter $u_i = v_j$. The set of k-candidates in Figure 1 is

$$(3,2),(9,6),(7,9),(4,11),(15,7),(11,9),(8,14),(5,15),$$
$$(19,8),(15,10),(12,13),(9,19),(14,14),(13,15),(17,16).$$

The basic strategy of the algorithm is to compute the set of all k-candidates and then collect an lcs from these (such an lcs clearly exists). The computation is done by performing a binary search, in a vector of at most n components, for certain matches, that is to say, pairs (i,j) for which $u_i = v_j$. Thus, r being the total number of matches this part of the algorithm takes time $O(r \log n)$ (we assume throughout that both input sequences have length n). The overall worst case time complexity of the algorithm is $O((r+n)\log n)$ and its space requirements are $O(q+n)$, where q is the total number of k-candidates encountered.

A key question is to investigate the total number q of candidates for particular pairs of sequences. This is interesting because $q \log n$ and q are lower bounds for the computing time and for the space requirements, once the present strategy is adopted. Unfortunately, there are pairs, such as $(abc)^n$ and $(acb)^n$ or $(abab)^n$ and $(abba)^n$ for which $q \in \Theta(n^2)$. Consequently, the derived upper bound can be obtained and the complexity of the algorithm is indeed $\Theta(n^2 \log n)$, that is the worst case behavior is even worse than that of the folklore algorithm.

The great advantage of this algorithm is that in the case of permutations the number r of matches is at most n, hence the algorthm works in time $O(n \log n)$. In actual practice the behavior of the algorithm is somewhere between these two bounds. Fortunately, most lines of true text files are either unique, or occur few times; hence, in practice this algorithm is definitely sub-quadratic! And this is why the algorithm works well even for long files (tens of tousands of lines).

One shortcoming of the algorithm of diff is that for families of pairs of sequences with $r \in \Theta(n^2)$ the running time is $\Theta(n^2 \log n)$ even if $q \in \Theta(n)$. There is at least one such family of files which occur in practice and for which diff behaves badly. These are files with many occurrences of one same line, say one fourth of the lines are blank. The easiest misbehavior of diff can be obtained by running it on sequences of the form ab^na and b^n [31].

Another shortcoming is that the computing time might depend on the order of specification of the sequences. Thus, computing the diff of $ab^{2n}a$ and b^n takes much longer than the diff of b^n and $ab^{2n}a$. The fact that the difference is not a symmetrical function does not justify this behavior because what dominates the running time is the computation of an lcs and an lcs does not depend on the order of the sequences.

Both these shortcomings disappear in an interesting variant discovered recently by Apostolico in [5]; see also [7]. This variant has time complexity $O((q+n) \log n)$ instead of $O((r+n) \log n)$. This is sufficient to guarantee an $O(n \log n)$ behavior, instead of $O(n^2 \log n)$, for files with only one frequent line, such as the example given above. However, the gain is obtained at the expense of complicated data structures, such as balanced binary search trees, and it is not clear whether the overhead of (always) using these structures is worth the time economy which is more accentuate only for special cases. Some experimentation might throw interesting light on this question.

A family which seems to defeat every known algorithm is given by pairs of random sequences over two letters. These seem to be the real "black sheeps" for sequence comparison; our luck is that they do not occur in practice very frequently. Or, do they? For instance, files that have many occurrences of two different lines in interlaced positions tend to behave as random sequences over two letters. These cases might arise in practice if we have blank lines with different indentations or two lines which occur frequently, such as the pairs **begin** and **end**.

Altogether, in spite of the excellence of diff, there seems to be ample

space for a substantially better algorithm, if only it could be found! But we
are hopeful that the proliferation of potentially equivalent quadratic algorithms is a sign that the ultimate word was not yet said.

ACKNOWLEDGEMENTS. The author thanks Christian Choffrut for inviting
him to Rouen where this work began and Dominique Perrin for insisting that
this survey be presented at the 1987 Ecole de Printemps at Ile d'Oléron. I
also wish to thank Alair Pereira do Lago who helped with the programming
tasks and with whom I maintained many interesting and helpful discussions
on the subject of this paper.

References

[1] A. V. Aho, D. S. Hirschberg, and J. D. Ullman. Bounds on the complexity of the longest common subsequence problem. *J. ACM*, 23:1–12,
1976.

[2] A. V. Aho, J. E. Hopcroft, and J. D. Ullman. *Data Structures and
Algorithms*. Addison-Wesley Pu. Co., Reading, MA, 1983.

[3] A. V. Aho, J. E. Hopcroft, and J. D. Ullman. *The Design and Analysis
of Computer Algorithms*. Addison-Wesley Pu. Co., Reading, MA, 1974.

[4] L. Allison and T. I. Dix. A bit string longest common subsequence
algorithm. *Inf. Process. Lett.*, 23:305–310, 1986.

[5] A. Apostolico. Improving the worst-case performance of the Hunt-
Szymanski strategy for the longest common subsequence of two strings.
Inf. Process. Lett., 23:63–69, 1986.

[6] A. Apostolico. Remark on the Hsu-Du new algorithm for the longest
common subsequence problem. *Inf. Process. Lett.*, 25:235–236, 1987.

[7] A. Apostolico and C. Guerra. The longest common subsequence problem revisited. *Algorithmica*, 2:315–336, 1987.

[8] R. M. Baer and P. Brock. Natural sorting over permutation spaces.
Math. Comp., 22:385–410, 1968.

[9] V. Chvátal, D. A. Klarner, and D. E. Knuth. *Selected combinatorial
research problems*. Technical Report STAN-CS-72-292, Computer Science Department, Stanford University, 1972.

[10] V. Chvátal and D. Sankoff. *Longest common subsequences of random sequences.* Technical Report STAN-CS-75-477, Computer Science Department, Stanford University, 1975.

[11] V. Chvátal and D. Sankoff. Longest common subsequences of two random sequences. *J. Appl. Prob.*, 12:306–315, 1975.

[12] M. Crochemore. Longest common factor of two words. In *Proceedings of CAAP'87, Pisa, Italy*, pages 26–36, 1987.

[13] J. Deken. Some limit results for longest common subsequences. *Discrete Math.*, 26:17–31, 1979.

[14] M. L. Fredman. On computing the length of longest increasing subsequences. *Discrete Math.*, 11:29–35, 1975.

[15] J. Gallant, D. Maier, and J. A. Storer. On finding minimal length superstrings. *J. Comput. Syst. Sci.*, 20:50–58, 1980.

[16] P. A. V. Hall and G. R. Dowling. Approximate string matching. *ACM Comput. Surv.*, 12:381–402, 1980.

[17] J. J. Hebrard. Distances sur les mots. Application à la recherche de motifs. Thèse de 3e cycle, Université de Haute-Normandie, 1984.

[18] P. Heckel. A technique for isolating differences between files. *Commun. ACM*, 21:264–268, 1978.

[19] D. S. Hirschberg. Algorithms for the longest common subsequence problem. *J. ACM*, 24:664–675, 1977.

[20] D. S. Hirschberg. An information theoretic lower bound for the longest common subsequence problem. *Inf. Process. Lett.*, 7:40–41, 1978.

[21] D. S. Hirschberg. A linear space algorithm for computing maximal common subsequences. *Commun. ACM*, 18:341–343, 1975.

[22] D. S. Hirschberg and L. L. Larmore. The set lcs problem. *Algorithmica*, 2:91–95, 1987.

[23] W. J. Hsu and M. W. Du. New algorithms for the LCS problem. *J. Comput. Syst. Sci.*, 29:133–152, 1984.

[24] J. W. Hunt and M. D. McIlroy. *An algorithm for differential file comparison*. Technical Report #41, Computing Science, Bell Laboratories, 1976.

[25] J. W. Hunt and T. G. Szymanski. A fast algorithm for computing longest common subsequences. *Commun. ACM*, 20:350–353, 1977.

[26] D. E. Knuth. *The Art of Computer Programming, Vol. 3, Sorting and Searching*. Addison-Wesley Pu. Co., Reading, MA, 1973.

[27] R. Lowrance and R. A. Wagner. An extension of the string-to-string correction problem. *J. ACM*, 22:177–183, 1975.

[28] D. Maier. The complexity of some problems on subsequences and supersequences. *J. ACM*, 25:322–336, 1977.

[29] W. J. Masek and M. S. Paterson. A faster algorithm computing string edit distances. *J. Comput. Syst. Sci.*, 20:18–31, 1980.

[30] K. Mehlhorn. *Data Structures and Algorithms 1: Sorting and Searching*. Springer-Verlag, Berlin, 1984.

[31] W. Miller and E. W. Myers. A file comparison program. *Software - Practice and Experience*, 15:1025–1040, 1985.

[32] A. Mukhopadhyay. A fast algorithm for the longest common subsequence problem. *Information Sciences*, 20:69–82, 1980.

[33] N. Nakatsu, Y. Kambayashi, and S. Yajima. A longest common subsequence algorithm suitable for similar text strings. *Acta Inf.*, 18:171–179, 1982.

[34] S. B. Needleman and C. D. Wunsch. A general method applicable to the search for similarities in the amino acid sequence of two proteins. *J. Molecular Biology*, 48:443–453, 1970.

[35] Y. Robert and M. Tchuente. A systolic array for the longest common subsequence problem. *Inf. Process. Lett.*, 21:191–198, 19885.

[36] D. Sankoff. Matching sequences under deletion/insertion constraints. *Proc. Nat. Acad. Sci. U.S.A.*, 69:4–6, 1972.

[37] D. Sankoff and J. B. Kruskal. *Time Warps, String Edits, and Macro-molecules: the Theory and Practice of Sequence Comparison*. Addison-Wesley Pu. Co., Reading, MA, 1983.

[38] S. M. Selkow. The tree to tree editing problem. *Inf. Process. Lett.*, 6:184–186, 1977.

[39] P. H. Sellers. An algorithm for the distance between two finite sequences. *J. Comb. Th. A*, 16:253–258, 1974.

[40] P. H. Sellers. On the theory and computation of evolutionary distances. *SIAM J. Appl. Math.*, 26:787–793, 1974.

[41] P. H. Sellers. The theory and computation of evolutionary distances: pattern recognition. *J. of Algorithms*, 1:359–373, 1980.

[42] T. G. Szymanski. *A special case of the maximal common subsequence problem*. Technical Report TR-170, Computer Science Lab., Princeton University, 1975.

[43] W. F. Tichy. The string-to-string correction problem with block moves. *ACM Trans. Comput. Syst.*, 2:309–321, 1984.

[44] S. M. Ulam. Some combinatorial problems studied experimentally on computing machines. In S. K. Zaremba, editor, *Applications of Number Theory to Numerical Analysis*, pages 1–3, Academic Press, apa, 1972.

[45] T. K. Vintsyuk. Speech discrimination by dynamic programming. *Kibernetika*, 4:81–88, 1968.

[46] R. A. Wagner and M. J. Fischer. The string-to-string correction problem. *J. ACM*, 21:168–173, 1974.

[47] C. K. Wong and A. K. Chandra. Bounds for the string editing problem. *J. ACM*, 23:13–16, 1976.

THE LEXICAL ANALYSIS OF FRENCH

Max Silberztein

Laboratoire d'Automatique Documentaire et de Linguistique[1],
Centre d'Etudes et de Recherches en Informatique Linguistique[2]

0. Introduction

Computers are increasingly used for text processing. Therefore, large amount of documents are stored at one point or another on magnetic supports, and thus can be used for computer or linguistic processing. Such available texts constitute basic linguistic material, hence, it is normal that linguists should try to use computer-based methods to analyze them.

Linguistic analysis at any level (whether syntactic or semantic) should not be started without a complete list of the words of the text with minimal grammatical information. Hence, compiling such an elementary lexicon is a necessery step in any linguistic analysis. The process of recognizing the words of a text is called **lexical analysis**. It requires purely computer-based calculations as well as consulting linguistic data bases. Building a lexical parser that recognizes the words of a text (without any approximation) is indispensable. For instance, it is not possible to analyze the sentence:

Il table sur les pieds noirs pour être élu
(He banks on the Algerian-born Frenchmen to be elected)

if one doesn't know that the token *table* (*banks*) can be a conjugated form of the verb *tabler* (*to bank*), and *pieds noirs* (*Algerian-born Frenchmen*) can be a compound noun.

Building a lexical parser requires that some linguistic problems be formulated within a formal framework. The lexical analysis can be seen as a projection of the tokens of a text into the system of dictionaries. A token is recognized when it is associated with the linguistic informations stored in the dictionaries of the system. On the one hand, an alphabetic representation must be defined for the dictionary. On the other hand, texts are available in a wide variety of typographic forms. One of the problems we address is the matching of the two representations of linguistic elements. We decompose this question in a large number of simple cases, each well-known. But the difficulty lies in the formalization of not always well-defined habits of writing, and in the interaction of all these elementary phenomena.

DELA is LADL's system of dictionaries. It contains the DELAS, the DELAF, the DELAP and the DELAC. DELAS is LADL's Electronic Dictionary for Simple words, which was constructed by Blandine Courtois (1987). It now contains 70,000 simple entries, with which are associated grammatical information (verb, noun, adjective, etc.) and morphological information indicating how verbs are conjugated and how nouns and adjectives are inflected. By using this morphological information, Blandine Courtois generated automatically the DELAF (LADL's Electronic Dictionary for inflected

---

[1]. Unit 819 of the CNRS. This work has been partly financed by the Programme de Recherches Coordonnées «Informatique Linguistique» of the Ministry of Research and Technology.
[2]. FIRTECH Industries de la langue française.

Forms) which contains 550,000 word forms, like *mangerions* (*we would eat*), *chaises* (*chairs*). The DELAP (LADL's Electronic Dictionary for Phonemics) has been constructed by Eric Laporte; it has the same entries as the DELAS, and associates with each entry a phonemic representation. The DELAC (LADL's Electronic Dictionary for Compound words) contains 60,000 compound words, like *pomme de terre*, *pied noir*. DELA has special provisions for handling proper names.

Formal definitions have to be given for the fundamental linguistic objects in order to recognize them:

Basic objects
1. Letters
2. Delimiters
2.1. Orthographic signs
2.2. Punctuation marks
2.3. Digits and symbols
Strings
1. Words
1.1. Simple words
1.2. Affixes
1.3. Abbreviations
1.4. Compound words
2. Numbers
3. Punctuation
4. Sentences

If the text is available only on paper, the 'basic' automatic recognition of the characters leads to unresolved problems; fortunately, we study texts available on computers, in which characters are already identified.

We describe in this paper some contextual constraints in French which are used for the automatic recognition of simple and compound words. These constraints can be represented in automata form, using a language similar to the LEX language ([M.E. Lesk and E. Schmidt, 1978]).

1. Basic objects

Computers process alphabetical, numerical, punctuation and semi-graphical characters. These characters are encoded in a normalized digital form (the most usual are ASCII and EBCDIC).

1.1. The letters

We first describe the alphabet used in the DELA system. We then describe the alphabet used in current French texts, and the problems which arise during the projection from the text into the DELA system.

1.1.1. The DELA alphabet

The DELA alphabet contains 45 letters:

a à á â ä ă b c ç d e è é ê ë f g h i j k l m n ñ o ó ô ö p q r s t u ù û ü v w x y z

Some of these letters are not usually considered to be French letters. However, they appear in foreign words which have been integrated into the French language. In the DELAS, the letter *á* appears in *soleá*, the letter *ä* appears in *minnesänger, tjäle*, the letter *ã* in *sertão, ñ* in *cañon, doña, señorita, ó* in *colón, ö* in *angström, föhn, gödéliser, maelström, öre, röntgen, röntgenthérapie, rösti, ü* in *capharnaüm, führer, günz, volapük, würm, würmien*[3].

Alphabetic order

The DELA system uses an alphabetic order which uses a two step comparison:

-- First, it erases the accents and scans the new words from left to right, using the order: $a < b < ... < z$. For example, to compare *été* and *enfant*, it first constructs *ete* and *enfant*. Then it compares the letters *t* and *n*; $n < t$, hence *enfant* < *été*.

-- If the two new words are equal, it scans the original words from left to right, using the following alphabetical order:

$$a < à < á < â < ä < ã, c < ç, e < è < é < ê < ë, n < ñ, i < î < ï, o < ó < ô < ö, u < ù < û < ü$$

For example, it obtains *relevé* < *relève*, since $e < è$. Note that this order is different from the one used in current dictionaries, in which $é < è$ and the scan of the second step is made **from right to left**, so that *relève* < *relevé* since $e < é$.

1.1.2. The text alphabet

We process texts which have not been specially composed for analysis. Hence, they must be normalized for the DELA system, because in addition to the letters already mentioned, current texts may include capital letters, ligatures and foreign letters.

Capital letters

Capital letters are used for syntactic and stylistic purposes. However, the entries of DELA dictionaries are in lowercase letters. Accessing the dictionaries requires that capitalized words be mostly rewritten in lower case. This rewriting is simple if there is a correspondence between lowercase and uppercase letters, that is, if every lowercase letter corresponds to an uppercase letter. In most French texts, accents are missing on capitals, in which case the program must use a special procedure in order to place the accent, and thus to find the right word (cf. 2.1.1.).

The ligatures

Ligatures (*æ* in *praesidium* and *œ* in *oeuf*) are used in high quality printed texts. It is only a matter of elegance. Some words are written with a ligature (*præsidium, œuf*), others not (*maestro, autoenchasser*), but there is no word in which the ligature has a syntactic or semantic meaning. Separating the two letters (*æ* -> *ae*) doesn't create any ambiguity, so a parser can be based on an alphabet which doesn't have the doubled letters.

Obviously, if the purpose of the parser is to check the texts in order to do high quality printing, it must distinguish the doubled letters.

---

[3]. The Académie decided in 1975 to put a diaeresis on the letter *u* in the following words: *aigüe, ambigüe, ambigüité, cigüe, exigüe, argüer, gagéüre, mangéüre, rongéüre, vergéüre*, etc. This reform has not yet been applied.

Foreign letters

If we process a text in which foreign letters can occur, they have to be translated. For example, we can write *angström* instead of *ångström*, and *ss* instead of the German *β*. For the non Latin languages, we may use the norms AFNOR or some of the recommendations ISO, or any other reference documents:

Cyrillic	*norm AFNOR NF Z 46-001*
Arabic	*norm AFNOR NF Z 46-001*
Hebrew	*norm AFNOR NF Z 46-001*
Greek	*recommendation project ISO/TC 46(315)*

e.g. [M.-L Dufour, 1971].

1.2. Delimiters

Delimiters are the extra characters used to separate strings of letters. For instance, blank, carriage return and comma are delimiters. Letters and delimiters in principle constitute disjoint sets. This feature leads to a great simplicity in the recognition of simple words. However, the apostrophe and the hyphen (Orthographic signs) may sometimes be considered as letters in a word, for example *aujourd'hui*, *clopin-clopant*, and sometimes as delimiters: *l'arbre*, *mange-le*.

1.2.1. Orthographic signs

1.2.1.1. The apostrophe

In French, the apostrophe (ASCII code 39) is used for different purposes. It may occur:

-- in a compound word: *aujourd'hui*, *O'Connors*,
-- in an elision: *l'arbre*,
-- as a quotation mark: *le 'donneur'*,
-- in the English possessive form: *un Levi's*, *chez McDonald's*,
-- in some foreign words: *le chi'isme*, *Roch 'Hodech*,
-- to represent the minute, angular unit: *angle de 10°35'*,
-- in the representation of spoken language: *v'là un aut' type!*
-- etc.

The three first uses of the apostrophe are processed in our lexical analyser. The processing of the other cases would require specific subroutines, as for example a syntactic analysis of angular measure terms.

Elision is a complex phenomenon which appears between the final and the initial letters of two words in contact. In that case, the final letter is replaced with an apostrophe, and is not followed by a delimiter.

Elided letters

The letters are *a*, *e*, *i* and *u* can undergo elision in a small number of French words. These are:

ce	c'est, ç'a été
de	d'abord
entre	entr'apercevoir
grand	grand'mère
je	j'aime

jusque	jusqu'ici
la	l'armée
le	l'arbre
lorsque	lorsqu'il
me	il m'énerve
ne	il n'énerve personne
presque	presqu'ici
prud	prud'homme
puisque	puisqu'ici
que	qu'ici
quelque	quelqu'un
quoique	quoiqu'elle
se	il s'est blessé
si	s'il vient
te	il t'a blessé
tu	t'arrives?

The letters *c, ç, d, j, l, m, n, s, t* don't always correspond to an elision:

'c' est la troisième lettre de l'alphabet
('c' is the third letter of the alphabet)

On the other hand, the words *aujourd, entr, jusqu, lorsqu, prud, presqu, puisqu, qu, quelqu, quoiqu* cannot be found alone, without an apostrophe.

Words following an elision

Such words have an initial vocalic syllable, they begin with an *a, e, h, i, o, u, y,* or the corresponding accented letters.

Some elided words have further constraints:

After *c'*, we find only the pronouns *en* or *y*, or the three conjugated forms of verb 'être' *est, était, étaient*, or the inflected form of auxiliary verb 'avoir' *eût (c'eût été)*. After *ç'*, we find only the conjugated forms of auxiliary verb 'avoir' *a (ç'a été)*, *avait (ç'avait été)*, *aurait (ç'aurait été)*.

After *entr'*, we find the noun *acte*, or one of the five following verbs in the infinitive, or conjugated in the simple tenses *aimer, apercevoir, appeler, avertir, égorger*.

After *grand'*, we can find a few nouns *chose, maman, mère, papa, peine, père, pitié, place, poste, route, rue, voile* and so on[4]. All the strings *grand'*+word are processed as compound words, and have been listed as such in our lexicon.

After *j'*, we find the pronouns *en, y*, or a simple or compound verb conjugated in the first person of singular.

After *m'* ou *n'*, we find the pronouns *en, y*, or a simple or compound verb.

After the pronoun *s'* (se), we find the pronouns *en, y*, or a simple or compound verb in the infinitive, or conjugated in the third person (singular or plural). After the conjunction *s'* (si), only the pronouns *il* or *ils* occur.

---

[4]. In 1932, the Académie replaced the apostrophe with a hyphen in all the compound nouns with *grand*. Nevertheless, they are often written with an apostrophe.

After *t'* (te), we find the pronouns *en, y,* or a simple or compound verb. The verb can be an infinitive or conjugated form. After *t'* (tu), we find only the pronouns *en, y,* or a simple or compound verb conjugated in the second person singular.

The other words are less constrained. After the determiner *l'*, we find:

-- a masculine or feminine noun (*l'arbre, l'aile*),
-- an adjective (*l'aimable femme*),
-- an adverb (*l'élégamment vêtue*),
-- a pronoun (*l'un ou l'autre*),
-- an interjection (*l'euréka*),

The word following the determiner *l'* can be a compound word, so it is possible to find:

-- a preposition (*l'à côté, l'entre deux guerres*),
-- a verb (*l'aller retour, l'allume cigare*).

On the other hand, we find only a simple or compound verb, or a pronoun *en* or *y* after the pronoun *l'* (*Luc l'appelle*). The words:

$$d', jusqu', lorsqu', presqu', puisqu', qu', quelqu', quoiqu'$$

also constrain their right environment.

Text normalization

The lexical parser checks the context of the apostrophes occurring in the text, and the right context of the words *aujourd, entr, jusqu, lorsqu, prud, presqu, puisqu, qu, quelqu, quoiqu.*

Certain kinds of constraints are processed in the automatic analysis. These constraints are recorded in specific automata, as follows:

-- the constraints on words; for example, the lexical parser checks that the word *aujourd'* is followed by the word *hui*:

$$aujourd'hui$$

-- the constraints on lemmatized forms; the lexical parser checks that the singular form of the noun following the word *entr'* is for example *apercevoir*:

$$entr' < apercevoir >$$

These two cases concern compound words.

-- the constraints on parts of speech; for example, a finite automaton ([D. Perrin, 1988]) checks that the word following the word *t'* is a verb:

$$t' < V >$$

-- the constraints of flexion; for example, the lexical parser checks that the verb following the word *j'* is conjugated in the first person singular:

$$j' < V\text{-}1s >$$

$<M>$ represents any word, $<MV>$ represents any word beginning with a vowel, $<cousin>$ represents the forms *cousin, cousine, cousins, cousines*, $<ADJ\text{-}fs>$ represents any feminine singular adjective, etc.

Remark

Processing the contextual constraints facilitates the later syntactic analysis, because it resolves many morphological ambiguities. For example, in the string *j'aide*, the word *j* cannot be anything but a pronoun (e.g. it cannot be a noun as in *j est la dixième lettre de l'alphabet*), and the word *aide* represents only the verb 'aider' conjugated in the first person singular (it cannot be the noun 'aide' as in *un aide de camp*, or in *une aide spontanée*).

It is necessary to check that the word following the apostrophe begins with a vowel. The lexical conditions required to check the phonemic context of elision have been studied in [E. Laporte, 1988a].

1.2.1.2. The hyphen

This character (ASCII code 45) is used in many different ways. It appears:

-- in compound words: *bas-relief, grosso-modo, Jean-François, J.-C*
-- after certain prefixes: *électro-métallique, sous-payer*
-- between a word and a particle: *ce gardien-là, cette personne-même*
-- in compound numbers: *trente-six, quatre-vingt-dix-huitième*
-- between a verb and following pronouns: *dit-il, allez-vous-en, va-t-on*
-- as a dash -- it is then doubled[5] --
-- to indicate an end-of-line cut in a single word (Hyphenation)
-- for stylistic purposes: *Cesse de jouer à Monsieur-je-sais-tout*
-- to simulate a broken speech: *Reviens di-rec-te-ment!*
-- to represent an interval between two numbers: *les années 1940-1960*
-- in mathematical formulas (minus sign or subtraction): *1 - 2 = (-1)*
-- as a graphical sign, to underline texts, or to draw horizontal lines:

Introduction

-- etc.

The six first cases will be discussed. Generally, hyphenation (the seventh case) is processed by the computer, and is then encoded with a special code. The other cases have to be examined in specific applications.

The hyphen in compound words

Compound words are currently being listed in the DELAC. Most of them are written without any hyphen:

acier trempé, avion de ligne, carte bleue, pomme de terre

a lot of compound words appear with or without a hyphen:

attrape(-)nigaud, moyen(-)âge, pied(-)noir

a few must contain one:

abat-jour, attaché-case, c'est-à-dire, contre-enquête

These are discussed in [M. Mathieu-Colas, 1987] and [L. Blumenthal, 1987].

---

[5]. If the computer system allows it, a different character is used for the dash, longer than the hyphen. The mathematical symbols (minus sign or subtraction) are then represented by a dash.

The analysis of the hyphen is based on two tests:

1. checking the context of every hyphen in the text,

2. checking every compound word of the text which requires an obligatory hyphen.

The second test poses the problem of how to recognize compound words. For example, the compound words *nord-est* and *peut-être* require a hyphen. Consider the sentences:

> *Le nord-est peut être devant nous.*
> *(North-East may be in front of us)*
>
> *Le nord est peut-être devant nous.*
> *(North is perhaps in front of us)*
>
> ° *Le nord est peut être devant nous.*

The third sentence contains two possible orthographic errors, but when one is corrected, the other is cleared. It is not possible to correct it by inserting a hyphen without making a syntactic and semantic analysis of the sentence and its context. This is a general phenomenon: it is possible to detect the absence of the hyphen only in non-homonymous compound words. We can detect errors like:

> *parce-que* instead of *parce que*,
> *clopin clopant* instead of *clopin-clopant*

When it is present, the hyphen disambiguates an ambiguous string, which is recognized as a compound word.

This kind of description may appear superfluous in the given examples, but this is not the case for the automatic recognition of technical terms in data retrieval systems.

Prefixes and particles

The hyphen may occur between a prefix and a word. For example:

> *anti-démocratique, pré-analyze, sous-payer*
> *oto-rhino-laryngologie, belgo-britannique*

It also appears between a word and a particle, such as: *-ci, -là, -né, -même*:

> *cette femme-là, dans cette rue-même*

The context of the prefixes is described in the same way as the context of elided words:

> *électro-* $<M>$ *, jusqu'* $<MV>$

The lexical parser processes the strings $<M>$-*chef*, $<M>$-*adjoint* and $<M>$-*clé* as compound words.

Compound numbers

The hyphen appears «*in the numbers that are compounded by addition, between elements which are less than one hundred*» [M. Grevisse and A. Goosse, 1986] :

vingt-cinq, quatre-vingts
°*deux-cents,* °*trois-mille-deux-cent-quatre*

The conjunction *et* can replace the hyphen in compound numbers (*quatre-vingt et un*). Grevisse's rule is not always followed in practice, since numbers less than one hundred are often found without a hyphen (*trente quatre*). The lexical parser processes the hyphen in cardinal or ordinal numbers less than one hundred:

la quatre-vingt-dix-septième personne
(*the ninety seventh person*)

Verbs followed by pronouns

One or two pronouns may be attached to a verb via hyphen. We distinguish two cases:

-- the verb is followed by its subject: *dis-je, déclaré-je, répondit-il, mange-t-on, est-ce*, etc. The lexical parser checks that the hyphen appears in one of the following schemas:

<V-1s>-je	*dis-je*
<V-2s>-tu	*dis-tu*
<V-3s>-(il+elle+on)	*dit-il*
<V-3s>-t-(il+elle+on)	*parle-t-il*
<être-3>-ce	*était-ce*
aurait-ce	*aurait-ce été*
<V-1p>-nous	*allons-nous*
<V-2p>-vous	*allez-vous*
<V-3p>-(ils+elles)	*viennent-ils*

Note that -*ce* occurs only after the verb 'être' conjugated in the third person, or after the form *aurait* of the verb 'avoir'. -*t* occurs only after a verb conjugated in the third person singular.

The following highly literary inflected forms are not presently treated in the DELAF: *chanté-je, parlé-je, dussé-je, eussé-je*, etc.

-- the verb in the imperative can be followed by one or two pronoun complements: *rendez-moi, donnez-la-lui*, etc. The description in the lexical parser is:

<V-Imp>-<PRO>-<PRO>	*donne-la-moi*
<V-Imp>-<PRO>'<PRO>	*donne-m'en*
<V-Imp>-t-<PRO>	*va-t-en*
<V-Imp>-<PRO>	*donnez-lui*

The first pronoun which follows the verb in the imperative present tense (marked *Imp* in the DELAF) can be elided (*donne-m'en*). The pronouns *en* and *y* have a specific use:

«*en* sometimes occurs in first position, this is not allowed in good French use: *Félicitons-en-le* [...]; *m'y* et *t'y* must be avoided...» [M. Grevisse and A. Goosse, 1986].

In *mènes-y-moi, vas-y*, etc., the verbs should be analyzed as conjugated forms in the second person imperative present (instead of *mène* and *va*); that information is not available in the DELAF. A natural solution could be a transduction of the information attached to the ending: second person singular of the indicative present tense becomes second person singular of the imperative.

It is not clear whether the word *en* in *allez-vous-en*, *viens-t-en*, etc. is a pronoun (it may be an interjection).

The partial description has important consequences with information already available in the DELA: strings like *aide-le* are disambiguated: *aide* cannot be anything but a verb in the imperative present tense, second person singular, and *le* cannot be anything but a pronoun. Consider the sentences:

> *Donne le tout à l'heure*
> *(Give all of it on time)*
>
> *Donne-le tout à l'heure*
> *(Give it in a few minutes)*

In the first sentence, *le* is a determiner; in the second, it is a pronoun. The word *le* in the first sentence cannot be recognized as a determiner without a complete syntactic analysis. In the second sentence, thanks to the hyphen, we can recognize *Donne* as a verb in the imperative present tense, and *le* as a pronoun.

1.2.2. Punctuation marks

We consider the following characters:

the blank, the comma «,», the period «.», the colon «:», the semi colon «;», the exclamation point «!», the question mark «?», points of suspension «...», brackets «(» and «)», the dash «--», a new paragraph, and quotation marks (double quotes) ««» and «»».

Special uses

The punctuation marks may be used in some special ways:

-- in the writing of numbers: *1.234.567,89*
-- the period is used for abbreviations: *etc. i.e.*
-- the period may occur to draw lines:

> *Chapitre 1.................................page 12*

or as delimiter, in codes, telephone numbers or dates: *43.37.01.01, le 1.7.79*
-- the colon represents mathematical division: *10 : 2 = 5*
-- the closing bracket and the period may appear in enumerations or in titles: *1.2.4. Conclusion, IV) Conclusion.*
-- etc.

Such special uses interfere with the punctuation, and complicate the lexical analysis.

1.2.3. Digits and symbols

The ten digits have to be represented unambiguously, as they are in ASCII and EBCDIC codes. The lexical parser is not designed to analyze texts in which the letter *O* and the digit *0* have the same code.

Certain graphic symbols can be used to represent words:

Symbols	Words
#	sharp
°	degree
$	dollar
&	and
£	pound (money)
§	paragraph
%	per cent

...

These symbols could be replaced with the corresponding words.

2. Words

The lexical parser tries to recognize words, numbers, punctuation and sentences. We describe in this paper the problems which arise in the recognition of words.

By words, we mean these linguistic objects which are associated with lexical information: morphological, syntactic, semantic, etc. The lexical analyzer must associate the tokens of the text with the lexical entries. The lexical analysis works with tokens as strings of characters; we distinguish different types of strings. There are the simple words, affixes, compound words, abbreviations and alphanumeric strings.

2.1. Simple words

We start from simple words which are contiguous strings of letters, as listed and described in the DELA system. The lexical parser processes three different categories of tokens:

-- lowercase simple words (*and, table*);
-- simple words with initial capital letter (*Beaucoup, Luc*), or simple words written entirely in capitals (*INTRODUCTION, IBM*);
-- more general forms of words:

McCarthy, FitsGerald
MemSoft, MicroVax
kW, ADNc, etc.

2.1.1. Recognition of uppercase words

We have seen that the uppercase letters are often unaccented. The letters *A C E I N O U* are then ambiguous in French. In order to recognize words which contain one of these letters, we have to look up a dictionary. For instance, to analyze the sentence:

Etant donné un ensemble de caractères

we have to know which of the words (*etant, ètant, étant, êtant* or *ëtant*) matches *Etant*. This case is a simple one: only *étant* is a French word. More difficult cases are frequently found. For example, there are words which differ only by an accent ([S. Woznika, 1988]):

a (verb 'avoir' or noun), à (preposition)
de (preposition), dé (noun), etc.

If one of these words occurs in unaccented uppercase letters, there is a lexical ambiguity. For example, in the sentence:

IL A DONNE LA CARTE
(HE HAS GIVEN THE MAP)

A is ambiguous (*a* or *à*), *DONNE* is ambiguous (*donne* or *donné*), *LA* is ambiguous (*la* or *là*), *CARTE* is ambiguous (*carte* or *carté*). During the lexical analysis, these ambiguities are processed in the same way as morphological ambiguities. For example, in the DELAF, the form *a* is associated with the morphological information:

a ((avoir V1:P3s)(a N2:Nms:Nmp))

which means that it represents either the verb *avoir* (*to have*) conjugated in the third person singular present, or the masculine noun *a* (singular or plural). The word *à* is associated with the information:

à ((à Pré))

which means that it is a preposition. The word *A* is then represented by:

A ((avoir V1:P3s)(a N2:Nms:Nmp)(à Pré)))

During the lexical analysis, the above text is then analyzed as follows:

IL((il Pro)) A((avoir V1:P3s)(a N2:Nms:Nmp)(à Pré)) DONNE((donner V3:P1s:P3s:S1s:S3s:Y2s)(donne N21:Nfs)(donné N1:Nms)(donné A32:Ams)(donner V3:Kms)) LA((la N2:Nms:Nmp)(la Dét)(la Pro)(là Adv)(là Int)) CARTE((carter V3:P1s:P3s:S1s:S3s:Y2s)(carte N21:Nfs)(carter V3:Kms))

2.1.2. Inflexion

Simple words are generally inflected in texts; thus, adjectives may appear in the feminine, nouns in the plural, verbs may be conjugated, etc. Linguistic information needed for parsing is stored in lexicons whose entries are in standard forms: verbs are represented by their infinitive form, nouns by their singular form, adjectives by their masculine singular form. Recognizing simple words requires morphological analysis in order to calculate the standard form. For instance, to analyze the sentence:

Les garçons vont au cinéma
(The boys go to the cinema)

one needs particular information about the noun *garçon* (*boy*) and the verb *aller* (*to go*). To perform the morphological analysis, we simply use the DELAF, which is automatically derived from the DELAS dictionary by inflecting all the forms. A sample of the entries in the DELAF is given in table 1.

2.1.3. Roman numerals

A roman numeral is a string of letters on the alphabet { c d i l m v x }. Roman numerals are found in lowercase (*xiv*) and in uppercase (*XIV*) but not in mixed case

(Xiv). During the lexical analysis of a text, the roman numerals are processed in the following manner:

$$XIV((XIV\ CR=14))$$

The word *C* is ambiguous, it is analyzed as follows:

$$C((c\ N2S:Nms:Nmp)(C\ CR=100))$$

2.1.4. Proper names

Proper names must be placed in a special dictionary of the DELA system. We have no significant dictionary of proper names. Recognizing a proper name automatically by analyzing its context requires a set of special procedures. For instance, words whose initial letter is capital are not always proper names:

Luc aime la Liberté
(Luc loves Freedom)

Il prend sa Carte Bleue
(He takes his Master Card)

Words that are not found in our dictionary and have a capital initial letter could be considered as proper names. Proper names can be homonymous with common words in the dictionaries (*Pierre, pierre*), in which case they require a complex analysis of their context.

2.2. Affixes

Affixed words may or may not have a hyphen after the affix: *anti-missile, antimissile*. Because of our formal point of view, these two cases are processed differently.

2.2.1. Affixes in words

Some strings -- traditionally considered compound words -- are processed as simple words: *dicarboxylique, électromagnétique*, etc. Hence, these words are listed in the DELAS. This solution facilitates the recognition of simple words, but increases the number of DELAS entries. For instance, it is possible to add the following prefixes in front of many verbs and of their derived forms:

auto, bi, co, de, dé, dis, dys, en, in, mé, re, ré, sub, sur, etc.

In the DELAS, these are independent entries:

autostructurer, déstructurer, restructurer,
redéstructurer, préstruturer, redéstructurer, etc.

This phenomenon of prefix iteration has numerous constraints, and hence, it cannot be described by general rules, and must be studied for each verb. [A. Dugas, 1988] has studied the use of the prefix *auto-* before verbs, [D. Leeman, 1988] has studied the adjectivization of French verbs that introduces the suffix *-able*. This kind of study will have to be carried out for other prefixes (*re, en, dé*, etc.) and other suffixes (*ique, iste*, etc.).

We describe now prefixes attached by a hyphen.

2.2.2. Prefixes

Some of the prefixes are free, i.e. they can occur as separate words:

Luc est non violent, Luc est pour la non-violence

Others do not occur alone (*sémantico-*). In general, strings such as *franco-belge* are not processed as compound words, because:

-- they are too numerous: for instance, given any two countries, we can describe their relations by writing one nationality in a prefix form (*les relations italo-américaines, germano-australiennes*, etc.),

-- their syntactic and semantic properties can be calculated from their constituents.

When a prefix appears only before a few words, for example *grand'*, we prefer to enumerate the strings, and process them as compound words.

Some independent affixes are numerous and have various semantic functions. We have:

anti-, archi-, au-, avant-, bi-, centi-, contre-, déca-, déci-, ex-, extra-, hecto-, inter-, intra-, kilo-, micro-, milli-, mono-, multi-, nano-, néo-, par-, pico-, pré-, pro-, pseudo-, quadri-, re-, ré-, self-, sous-, supra-, tri-, ultra-, uni-, vice-

chimico-, informatico-, logico-, psycho-, sémantico-, socio-, afro-, américano-, belgo-, euro-, germano-, italo-, etc.

In order to generate as many prefixes as possible, we have studied the words in *-ique* and the names of countries. Whenever possible, we generated the corresponding prefix:

Words	Prefixes
logique	*logico-*
psychique	*psycho-*
...	
Amérique	*américano-*
Chine	*sino-*
France	*franco-*
Espagne	*hispano-*
Union soviétique	*soviéto-*

...

Unfortunately, it is very often difficult to decide whether such a generated prefix belongs to French. For example, to describe the relations between Alsace and Auvergne, is it possible to write *les relations alsaço-auvergnates*, or *les échanges auvergno-alsaciens* ?

2.2.3. Dual entries

A word such as *deltaplane* is a DELAS entry, its variant *delta-plane* is a DELAC entry independant of the previous one. Hence, we must reserve a special treatment for such words which can appear either as simple or as compound words. In French, the rule is to attach the prefix *sur* ('*over*') to verbs, and to use a hyphen for the prefix *sous-* ('*under*'). This difference implies that the verb *suralimenter* is processed as a simple verb.

and the verb *sous-alimenter* is processed as a compound one. Normally, such forms should be represented by an automaton (cf. Gross M. in the present volume):

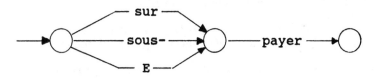

2.3. Abbreviations

We distinguish three kinds of abbreviations:

-- abbreviations which have become simple words (*le métro, 3 km, la BNP*);
-- abbreviations which are written with one or more periods (*etc., i.e.*);
-- more complex abbreviations, in which the length and the position of the letters change (*M^r, Mme, S^t*) or in which there are non alphabetic characters (*n°*).

The first kind of abbreviations are processed as simple words, and are stored in the DELAS (except for the proper names). The third kind of abbreviations could be processed in relation with a specific application. The following are abbreviations that we currently process:

c.-à-d. (*c'est-à-dire*), *cf.* (*confer*), *chap.* (*chapitre*), *col.* (*colonne*), *coll.* (*collection*), *éd.* (*édition*), *e.g.* (*par exemple*), *et al.* (*et alii*), *etc.* (*et caetera*), *ex.* (*exemple* or *exercice*), *fig.* (*figure*), *ibid.* (*ibidem*), *i.e.* (*id est*), *id.* (*idem*), *m.* (*monsieur*), *n.b.* (*nota bene*), *n.d.l.r.* (*note de la rédaction*), *n.d.t.* (*note du traducteur*), *op. cit.* (*opus citatum* or *opere citato*), *p.* (*page*), *pp.* (*pages*), *p.s.* (*post scriptum*), *t.* (*tome*), *vol.* (*volume*), *w.-c.* (*water-closet* =*toilet]*)

More specific abbreviated terms could be included in the system (*ms.* for *manuscrit*, *v.* for *verset*, etc.).

2.4. Compound words

Compound words are numerous in texts. Their syntactic functions have no relation to their compound characters:

Adjective	*bleu-ciel, haute fidélité*
Adverb	*à gorge déployée, de toute façon*
Conjunction	*par conséquent, c'est-à-dire*
Determiner	*la plupart, les trois quarts*
Noun	*Moyen-âge, pomme de terre*
Verb	*tenir compte, avoir lieu*

Gaston Gross has evaluated the number of compound nouns as approximately 300,000, whereas only about 20,000 are found in current dictionaries. These words must be listed *in extenso* because their syntactic and semantic properties cannot be predicted. For instance, *une deux chevaux* is a car, *un pied noir* is a person, the verbal form *rendez-vous* is a noun, etc. ([G. Gross, 1986]).

Compound nouns have been studied in [G. Gross, R. Jung and M. Mathieu-Colas, 1987]; Compound verbs, adjectives and adverbs have been studied in [M. Gross, 1986, 1988].

2.5.1. Inclusions and transformations

Compound words which accept inclusions and/or transformations are not recognized in the texts. Most of them are compound verbs:

> *(avoir lieu) le cours a toujours lieu dans cette salle*
> *(to take place) the lesson takes always place in this room*

Some adverbs pose several problems of a similar kind ([M. Gross, 1988]):

> *Pour les beaux yeux de quelqu'un*: *Luc est venu pour les beaux yeux de (Paul+son chef)*, *Luc est venu pour tes beaux yeux*.

> *For the sake of somebody*: *Luc came for the sake of (Paul+his boss)*, *Luc came for your sake*.

[E. Laporte, 1988b] has shown that their recognition requires full syntactic analysis of the sentence.

2.5.2. Recognition of compound words

Automatic recognition of compound words means that we only signal to the syntactic parser the possibility of the presence of a compound word ([A. Bérard-Dugourd and G. Richard, 1986]). For instance, the string *cordon bleu* is described in the DELAC dictionary, hence is recognized as a compound noun every time it occurs in a text. It is necessary to make a syntactic (even a semantic) analysis of the sentence to know whether it represents a compound word ('a good cook'), or an ordinary phrase ('a blue cord'). When we use the term *compound word recognition*, we always mean *recognition of the possibility that a string represents a compound word*.

The recognition is done in two steps. First, every simple word is looked up in the DELAC dictionary. If a word is an entry of DELAC, we use the associated automaton to check the context. For example, to analyze the sentence:

> *Il mange une pomme de terre brûlée aujourd'hui*

we look up in the DELAC every simple word: *il, mange, une, pomme, de, terre, brûlée, aujourd*, and *hui*. A sample of the entries of the DELAC is given in table 2. We find that only *pomme, terre* and *aujourd* are keys of the DELAC. We check the context of these words, and recognize the compound words *aujourd'hui, pomme de terre* and *terre brûlée*. The result given by the lexical parser looks like:

> *Il mange une [1pomme de [2terre]1 brûlée]2 [3aujourd'hui]3*

Resolving such indexed parenthesis delimitate the possible compounds; it will require syntactic calculations.

3. Conclusion

The automatic linguistic analysis of texts requires basic information about the simple and compound words of the text. Lexical analysis is the preliminary step before syntactic analysis. We have shown that important linguistic problems appear during this basic step. Some of them cannot yet be solved (recognition of proper names, compound verbs, and so on); others, if solved during lexical analysis, facilitates the syntactic analysis by reducing the degree of ambiguity of the text.

The lexical parser is based on a program (automaton) which could be used in more general cases in order to disambiguate some strings. For example, we have described the context of the string *j'*; in the same way, it would be possible to describe the context of the word *je*, which appears only in a limited number of schemas.

We have given an enumeration of problems that have to be solved in order to recognize words. Each of these problems is well-known. What we have attempted here is to formulate them in such a form that they can be represented by finite automata and treated by the corresponding algorithms. It should be clear that the number of automata to be built, their size and the formulation of their interaction is by no mean trivial: a complex program is required simply to recognize the words of a text.

Table 1: First entries of the DELAF dictionary

%a,avoir.V1:P3s,a.N2:Nms:Nmp
%à,à.Pré
%ab,ab.Xin
%abaca,abaca.N1:Nms
%abacas,abaca.N1:Nmp
%abacule,abacule.N1:Nms
%abacules,abacule.N1:Nmp
%abaissa,abaisser.V3:J3s
%abaissable,abaissable.A31:Ams:Afs
%abaissables,abaissable.A31:Amp:Afp
%abaissai,abaisser.V3:J1s
%abaissaient,abaisser.V3:I3p
%abaissais,abaisser.V3:I1s:I2s
%abaissait,abaisser.V3:I3s
%abaissâmes,abaisser.V3:J1p
%abaissant,abaisser.V3:G00,abaissant.A32:Ams
%abaissante,abaissant.A32:Afs
...

Table 2: First entries of the DELAC dictionary

%a
*/postérieur:un:ms:NA
*/privatif:un:ms:NA
%abandon
*/de/famille:un:ms:NDN
*/de/poste:un:ms:NDN
%abaque
*/cartésien:un:ms:NA
%abattage
*/à/la/cognée:un:ms:NAN
*/à/la/scie:un:ms:NAN
*/clandestin:un:ms:NA
*/rituel:un:ms:NA
%abattement
*/à/la/base:un:ms:NAN
*/fiscal:un:ms:NA
...

References

Bérard-Dugourd Anne and Richard Gilles, 1986. *Le traitement des locutions dans l'analyse du langage naturel.* Centre scientifique IBM France, Paris.

Blumenthal Lucie, 1987. *Le trait d'union dans les mots composés du français.* Mémoires du CERIL, Evry.

Courtois Blandine, 1987. *DELAS: Dictionnaire Electronique du LADL pour les mots Simples du français.* Rapport technique du LADL, Université Paris 7.

Dufour M.-L, 1971. *Le tapuscrit, recommandations pour la présentation et la dactylographie des travaux scientifiques.* Ecole des hautes études en sciences sociales, Paris.

Grevisse Maurice and Goosse André, 1986. *Le bon usage,* douxième édition. Editions Duculot, Paris-Gembloux.

Gross Gaston, 1986. *Typologie des noms composés.* Rapport A.T.P. Nouvelles recherches sur le langage, Paris XIII, Villetaneuse.

Gross Gaston, Jung René and Mathieu-Colas Michel, 1987. *Noms composés.* Rapport n°5 du Programme de Recherches Coordonnées «Informatique Linguistique», Université Paris 7.

Gross Maurice, 1986. *Les adjectifs composés du français.* Rapport n°3 du Programme de Recherches Coordonnées «Informatique Linguistique», CNRS, Paris.

Gross Maurice, 1989. *Grammaire transformationnelle du français: 3 Syntaxe de l'adverbe* Cantilène, Paris.

Laporte Eric, 1988a. *Méthodes algorithmiques et lexicales de phonétisation de textes, Applications au français.* Thèse de doctorat en informatique, LADL, Université Paris 7.

Laporte Eric, 1988b. *La reconnaissance des expressions figées lors de l'analyse automatique.* Langages n°90: «Les expressions figées». Larousse, Paris.

Leeman Danièle, 1988. *Echantillons des adjonctions au DELAS d'adjectifs en -able* Rapport du Programme de Recherches Coordonnées «Informatique Linguistique» LADL, Université Paris 7.

Lesk M.E. and Schmidt E., 1978. *Lex - A Lexical Analyzer Generator.* Bell Laboratories Murray Hill, New Jersey 07974.

Mathieu-Colas Michel, 1987. *Variations graphiques de mots composés.* Rapport n°4 du Programme de Recherches Coordonnées «Informatique Linguistique», CNRS, Paris.

Perrin Dominique, 1989. *Automates et algorithmes sur les mots,* Annales de Télécommunications, CNET, Paris.

Woznika Stan, 1987. *Dictionnaire des homographes du français.* Rapport de recherche du LADL, Université Paris 7.